CHARACTER AWARENESS

BY **ALEXANDREA SIMS**

WITH **DAN CLARK**

IZZARD INK
—PUBLISHING—

Published by Izzard Ink Publishing

Character Awareness

©Copyright 2017 Alexandrea Sims.

ISBN: 9781630729318

All rights reserved. No part of this book may be reproduced or utilized, in any form or by any means, electronic or mechanical, without prior permission in writing from the publisher.

Table of Contents

Acknowledgements 5

Preface 9

Must Read Introduction: CHARACTER AWARENESS . . . 11

Chapter One: CLARITY 21

Chapter Two: HONESTY 35

Chapter Three: ANTI-BULLYING 49

Chapter Four: RESPONSIBILITY 59

Chapter Five: ADDICTION PREVENTION 67

Chapter Six: CONSISTENCY 79

Chapter Seven: THWARTING SUICIDE 87

Chapter Eight: EXCELLENCE 105

Chapter Nine: RESILIENCY 119

About The Author. 133

Co-Author 135

Acknowledgements

WHAT INSPIRES YOU? That's the question I've asked myself since I was a little girl. With a passion for sports, activities, art and culture, and an unquenchable thirst for wisdom and understanding, there is no way I would have been inspired and qualified to write this book without some specific influences and role models in my life:

Thanks to my gymnastics coach Missy Marlow, who as a member of the U.S. Olympic Team, took me under her wing at five years of age and coached me for eight years until I competed in the national finals. Because of Missy I know why and how to face my fears, stay focused, push myself beyond my limits and be resilient.

Thanks to my first dance teacher Laura King Spinning, who taught me 'good' is never good enough, and that there is a difference between dancing and performing – a difference between 'marking the steps' and feeling the music so it flows through my movements. I now realize that this is the secret to having authentic relationships and living a wonderful, passionate and fulfilling life!

I owe an un-payable debt of gratitude to the owner of my dance studio, Kim DelGrosso, who founded and orchestrates the operations at the world renowned 'Center Stage,' where many of the professional dancers seen in Hollywood movies, Las Vegas productions, and on Dancing With The Stars learned and perfected their incredible skills. During the five years I studied at Center Stage Kim not only taught me the importance of being sophisticated, elegant, and polished on and off the stage, but she provided opportunities to compete in the most prestigious national competitions, which gave me the confidence I needed to move to Los Angeles and turn my dream of becoming a professional dancer into a reality.

Thanks to the extraordinary choreographer Nancy Omera, who believed in me as an 18 year old girl, and taught be responsibility by sending me on my first world tour where I performed for hundreds of thousands of fans throughout North and South and Central America. I will be forever grateful for this chance of a lifetime that changed the trajectory of my career forever!

Thanks to BLOC – one of the premier 'Talent Agencies" in the world, who represent me as a professional dancer and as an actress in commercials and film. They are extraordinary at every level and incredible in the way they use their powerful reputation to connect me with awesome opportunities that I could never image!

I especially dedicate this book to my parents – first to my mom who has always lead by example and is the person whom I aspire to be - who shaped me into the person I am today, and taught me every valuable lesson necessary to be a decent human being. She is the most beautiful woman in the world – both inside and out! And to my Dad - who has always made me laugh and think and feel and help me understand that the purpose of life is not to get, to have, or to do. It is to 'become' everything I was born to be. Because of him I dream big and follow my heart, I never give up, I know it's not what happens, but what I do with what happens that defines who I am, and I realize that when I work hard anything is possible – even writing a book!

I also thank the incredible Dr. Kathy Bitner PhD, who as an exceptionally effective, well respected and admired school counselor created the 'Discussion Questions' included in each chapter to assist educators, coaches, parents and fellow counselors in facilitating in-classroom conversations about the nine different topics covered in this book.

And from the technical side of publishing I thank my amazing editor Katharine Goodman for polishing my pros and conjugating my verbs, my creative book designer Jimmy Sevilleno and publisher

Bob Howland for planting and watering the seed that I had the credibility to illuminate the significance of Character Awareness in a way that will help mold the minds and hearts of young people across our world.

Preface

THIS BOOK HAS been created especially for educators, school counselors, coaches, parents and students as a "Resource Book" to help you facilitate and guide conversations on the nine elements/qualities/attitudes, attributes, and traits of Character.

Each chapter is a stand-alone essay that allows the facilitator to interrupt the general flow of a curriculum package, lesson plan, or weekly routine to talk with students and children about one of the nine specific topics.

Pay particular attention to the list of "Discussion Questions" included at the end of each chapter that will stimulate appropriate conversation, debate, and the sharing of personal examples related to the topic.

Research proves that Character Awareness and Development is the one-stop-shop answer to every challenge facing our youth and schools today!

Must Read Introduction

CHARACTER

AWARENESS

When you think of character, what first comes to mind
Do you start to soul search to see what you'll find
Look deep down inside you and find what makes you tick
So when you're making choices, you'll know which one to pick

Will you take the high road and be honest, true and kind
Or take the path of least resistance running through your mind
Character is something that can always be improved
Take some notes and know that it is time to make a move

Time to finally be yourself, each day, so you will see
It's Character that makes you everything you're born to be!

(Copyright Alexandrea Sims 2017)

When I was invited to write a book on Character Awareness, my first reaction was a lack of self-confidence, questioning what a 25-year-old woman could possibly teach the world about anything? This, however, quickly turned into a positive response realizing that character development has nothing to do with age, gender, ethnicity, or culture. Every one of us should become a person of character, and fortunately, I was raised in five environments that taught me, tutored me, and expected me to live my life with character.

At home, I was taught that the only person I needed to be better than, was the person I was yesterday! And I was taught to be polite, humble, reverent, kind and committed to doing the right thing simply because it's the right thing to do.

When I arrived at school, I was expected to show respect for others, respect for learning, respect for property, and respect for authority. After school, I took gymnastics classes and dance lessons where it became obvious that inspired people don't have to be motivated. Which was evident in my neighborhood filled with parents, families, and good friends, for we all shared the same core values of integrity, service before self and a commitment to excellence in all we do.

Yes, I know these five environmental influences might sound unreal to you and your friends. But they should never sound unachievable!

Winners are not born, they are made. Leaders are not born, they are made. Neighborhoods and friendships are not discovered, they are created. No one is born with character. We develop it as we become more aware of what, how, where, when and why it's the backbone of every person, family, school, team and community.

The Beginning

Webster's dictionary defines Awareness as: "The act of becoming clear on what 'is,' what 'was,' and what 'could be,' devoid of any opinions and all prejudice. We see 'it' for what it is, nothing more, nothing less, 'it' just 'is.' Awareness of this whole truth means that regardless of what we have been conditioned to believe, there are not two sides to every story – only one, which is the whole and complete truth.

In other words, some things are true whether you believe them or not; everybody is entitled to an opinion, but nobody is entitled to the wrong facts. Only when you know the whole truth, can the truth make you free.

The dictionary defines Character as: "One's reputation, personal commitment to moral excellence – the combination of distinctive qualities and ethical traits."

As I interviewed many experts on the subject of character, I chose to collaborate with New York Times Best-Selling Author Dan Clark. His incredible reputation preceded him, his experience is vast and diversified, and his illustrative stories and wisdom will make the chapter topics come alive. For example, when I asked Dan to define character development in terms that every teenager and adult could comprehend, he distilled it into three of his most profound quotes:

"It is not enough to say, 'I will do my best.' We must succeed in doing that which is necessary."

"Under pressure, you don't step up your game. You succumb to the level of your preparation, training, and practice. Which means the pressure is not something that is naturally there. It is created when you question your own ability. When you know what you have been trained to do, there is never any question. That's why you train and practice so hard!"

"Crisis does not make or break the person – it just reveals the true character within."

My Personal Development

In light of these three fundamental truths, it is crystal clear that some things cannot be taught. You must learn them through personal experience. Character is one of those things. In other words, it is not enough to be motivated – we must *do* motivated. We can't just be empathetic and be strong – we must *do* empathetic and *do* strong. It's easier to act our way into positive thinking than to think our way into positive action.

Looking back, I became cognizant of this at the age of five-years-old when my parents gave me the opportunity to get involved in gymnastics. Six days a week, for two hours a day, for eight years in a row, I *"did"* character.

No, everybody did not get a trophy. Yes, there were winners and losers, the exhilarating thrill of victory and the devastating agony of defeat. But all in all, regardless of the outcome of each meet, my teammates and I discovered that exhaustion is acceptable, failing and falling are acceptable, crawling is acceptable, puking is acceptable, blood, sweat, and tears are acceptable. Even disappointment, discouragement, and sadness are acceptable, but whining, blaming, complaining and quitting are not. You can't quit – it's a league rule.

To make this long story shorter, my hard work and focused dedication paid off, as I was the State Champion several times and took second in the All-Around competition at Nationals as a twelve-year-old. More important than winning, however, is that I discovered the basic tenants of Character founded in the firm conviction that attitude is a choice – when your attitude is right, your abilities will always catch up. When you fail or fall, you must get up, refocus, face the vault, climb back on the beam or bars to complete your routine, and finish what you started. It is not what happens to you that defines who you are; it is what you do with what happens to you that defines who you are; you will never know how strong you are until you are tested and being strong is your only choice.

Gymnastics taught me discipline (which is minding someone else because they expect it), self-discipline (which is minding myself because I demand it), work ethic (to push myself and do hard things), and personal responsibility (which is knowing that it is what I do when my parents and coaches and teachers are not around that makes me a champion).

Now that I'm older, it's exciting and rewarding to recognize how developing these character traits at a young age has paid off in helping me minimize my mistakes, rise to the occasion in crisis situations as an adult, and better understand the deeper meaning of Character when taught in the simplest ways. Let me explain.

Road Signs And Warnings

One evening while driving along a mountainous road I was suddenly caught in a driving rainstorm. In a downpour punctuated with frequent claps of thunder and flashes of lightning, I could barely see the road – neither in front of me nor to the right or the left. This meant that I watched the white lines on that road more intently than ever before. Staying within the lines kept me from going onto the shoulder, and into the deep canyon on one side, and helped me avoid a head-on collision on the other side.

Would a right-thinking person deviate to the left, or the right, of a traffic lane if she knew the result would be fatal? If she valued her life, certainly she would stay between the lines.

As I drove that evening, I also noticed road signs that had been strategically placed to regulate my thinking and behavior, minimizing my chances of having an accident, so that I could arrive at my destination safely.

Stride To Be Better

The second illustrative experience happened when I was in Hawaii on vacation with my family. We were sitting in a pool when my dad's friend Naomi Rhode taught us all about Character Awareness. She and her husband, Jim, had been walking along the beach for several hundred yards when she paused to look back to see how far they had gone. She noticed their footprints in the sand and was immediately filled with pride. She pointed them out to her husband and commented, "Wow, think about how many times we have left our footprints in the lives of others."

Suddenly the ocean interrupted by sweeping in and washing away their footprints, leaving no sign they had ever been there. Naomi was puzzled and almost hurt. She asked her husband, "How can we leave a more lasting impression on people that will not be washed away with time?" He wisely replied, "Just walk on higher ground."

Life Is A Dance

Because I had obeyed the training rules and the rules of competition, which required that I stayed in between the lines in my tumbling routines, I became the state gymnastics champion several times acquiring a passion for dance in the Floor Exercise. Gratefully, my parents provided me an opportunity to add dance classes to my gymnastics practices, which eventually spawned into a burning desire to pursue hip-hop, ballroom, tap, contemporary and jazz. Over time, I followed my heart, left gymnastics, and discovered that life is a dance.

I love to dance. I love to take dance classes and teach others to dance. In fact, it is through dance that I untangle the complexities of life, comprehending my purpose and place in this world. Consequently, I love music – all kinds of music – from R&B to rock and roll, classical to jazz and pop, and because of my sister's influence I even like country. (Ha!) In fact, it is through the lyrics in two country songs that I sum up my feelings:

In the song called 'The Dance,' Garth Brooks sings:

> *Looking back, on the memory of*
> *The dance we shared beneath the stars above*
> *For a moment all the world was right*
> *How could I have known, you'd ever say goodbye*
> *And now, I'm glad I didn't know*
> *The way it all would end, the way it all would go*

Character Awareness

Our lives, are better left to chance, I could have missed the pain
But I'd of had to miss the dance.

In the song 'I Hope You Dance,' Lee Ann Womack sings:

Promise me that you'll give faith a fighting chance
And when you get the choice to sit it out or dance
I hope you dance.

Ever since I was twelve-years-old, I have been taking dance classes, private dance lessons, and competing on a national scale as part of the world-renowned dance studio Center Stage – responsible for training many of the world's most successful dancers including Derek Hough, Ashley DelGrosso, Jenna Johnson and Julianne Hough – featured on television's *Dancing With The Stars*, *So You Think You Can Dance*, *World of Dance*, in the biggest shows in Las Vegas, and in mega-hit movies like *La La Land*. In every dance competition, each individual dancer and ballroom couple, or studio team, is judged on three criteria: Technical Skill, Performance, and Content. The winner of the competition has the highest combined score of the three elements.

Technical Skill, Performance, Content

Technical Skill is the technique – the finely tuned skill set that allows you to execute a task or movement at the highest level of proficiency. Technically, you are doing each dance step correctly with perfectly straight feet, straight legs, pointed toes, constant traction, centered in your turns, and synchronizing movement and speed between partners. It is the skill with which you do your job. The skill that can only be achieved through strict obedience to specific rules of balance and principles of energy, followed by a relentless rehearsal schedule until you perfect each movement, one at a time, only to "clean" the dance for a four-minute performance.

Scoring high in Technical Skill begins when you know what happens after you tuck this and tighten that, with a perfect posture and what happens when this muscle moves, which is connected to that body part, to connect one movement toward the next in a beautiful fluid motion. In living life to the fullest and becoming everything you were born to be, these skills include being a good neighbor and a great friend. Technical Skill is achieved when your mind, body, thoughts, words, intentions, and behaviors are all in alignment. In other words, if the things you think about and believe in are different than the things you do, you will never be happy or at peace with yourself. Technical Skill is a focus on yourself and what you do.

Performance is the connection you have with the audience. Your Performance is what makes your practiced and polished Technical Skill come alive!

If you're an amazing dancer, you could do the most basic routine but make it amazing. It is the way you hold a pose, the way you simply look with intensity, move quickly, and the passion and meaning you bring to the moment that gives it value. The real pros can make the same move, and by simply changing their eyes and their attitude, alter their connection with the audience.

Extraordinary dancers know there is a difference between going through the mediocre motions of merely marking the choreographed steps, versus letting the music take you to a place where you passionately interpret it through movement. Extraordinary musicians know there is a difference between merely playing the notes, versus becoming the instrument and passionately sharing the emotional message the composer wanted us to feel and hear. Which one are you?

Just as the Performance of a professional dancer or musician can change negative energy in a room to positive energy and literally alter the atmosphere and tone of an event, so likewise, can you change the attitude and expectations of people around you, by genuinely serving and helping them to do the right thing simply because it is the right thing to do. Performance is a focus on your audience – on others.

Content is the actual dance number or piece of music that you choose, or someone else chooses for you to perform. It is the moment of truth when you decide to either push yourself beyond your past best personal performance or take the easy road of a complacent minimum requirement. Content has a hello and a goodbye – a beginning and an end to the assignment, so you know when and where to start, and when you are finished. Most importantly, Content is clarifying the purpose of the task – the "why" you are dancing or playing music, which dictates the specific Technical Skill required to accomplish the task, and the necessary motivation to want to perform it to the best of your ability.

With all due respect, I know there are a lot of dancers, musicians, and friends who are very good at what they do – technically – and every day they come to dance class, or to school as students, or work as teachers and coaches, and they perform putting in their required time and do a great job. Then they return the next day, and again do a great job – but the same job, to the same level of performance. Sadly, because of the minimum-requirement society in which we live, this is acceptable to many of our leaders, teachers, coaches, and parents.

My question: Is it acceptable to you? If so, why? And as it relates to character development and awareness, could it be that we all have been inundated with mediocrity for so long that we don't know the difference?

'Desensitized'

Because every human being on earth is born with a conscience, our conscience will never fail us. Only our desire to follow it decreases as we continue to make bad choices and do the wrong thing. I learned this one day when my friends and I walked into a room that stunk so bad our eyes started to water, triggering an automatic gag reflex that pushed us to the verge of throwing up. But when we stayed in that rank, repulsive room for ten minutes, suddenly it didn't stink anymore. It was now the new "normal." We had become "desensitized" to the subpar environment, and without even realizing it we had lowered our standard of performance excellence and had "settled" for less than the best.

I remember learning a scientific explanation of why and how this occurs when I was in Middle School. It's called the Second Law of Thermodynamics, which ironically illustrates the significant role environment plays in our Character Development stating: When you put freezing cold water into a vat of scalding hot water, in a matter of moments they amalgamate and morph into a warm, neutral temperature that is the average of the two. Can you relate this to any of the relationships you currently have in your life?

Have you been subconsciously and gradually desensitized by the T.V. shows you watch, the music you listen to, the over playing of video games, the magazine fashion trends, and the "pop culture" your friends claim as "cool?" Have you noticed how over the years, the standard of excellence in television censorship and movie ratings continually becomes more lenient?

Because this is a book only about Character Awareness, we are not passing moral judgment on these changes – only reminding everyone they are constantly going on, and a direct reflection on the character of those making the decisions.

Bottom Line

For this reason, I present to you the nine letters of the word C.H.A.R.A.C.T.E.R. as an acronym template wherein we discuss the nine elements of Character that will produce better Technical Skills that are required for you to be an outstanding student, a champion athlete, and/or an extraordinary dancer/musician/artist; produce better Content that pushes you to reach your full physical, mental and emotional potential; and create better Performances at home, at school, at work, at play - in the classroom, at your practices, in your games, and during your recitals, that will showcase your best version of yourself as you elevate and emulate Character Awareness for your family and friends. Cheers.

Chapter One

Character

Clarity

Sometimes in our lives, we get confused along the way
It's hard to see which path is right, and which one goes astray
If friends are misbehaving and they try to bring you down
Stay true to you, be bold, and never let them steal your crown

When life presents a test, and it is time for you to take
The only way to pass is when you learn from your mistakes
Always trust your values, and never change your views
Just be clear with every goal, and to yourself stay true.
(Copyright Alexandrea Sims 2017)

Clarity is defined in the dictionary as: "The quality of being easily understood in a very exact way; focused on purpose; being easily seen or heard; free from obscurity; the comprehensibility of clear expression with the adequate practical application tools required to implement what you know and see."

My personal definition is much simpler: 'We don't see things as they are - we see things as we are.' If you and I and a group of your friends were all inside looking out the same window at a lashing Los Angeles rainstorm, and someone complained, "What a horrible day," and someone else exclaimed, "What a wonderful day," the weather did not change! Attitude really is everything. Only when your attitude is right will your abilities catch up.

I remember when my high school friend was diagnosed with cancer and given only six months to live. To help her prepare for the fight of her life, the doctor asked her, "Is there a difference between dying of cancer and living with cancer? Yes? What's it going to be for you?" Because of her positive attitude that brought Clarity to why she wanted to out live the doctors prognosis, she lived for another six wonderful and rewarding years!

The significance of character development cannot reveal itself until we become crystal clear on who we are and why we are? Author Mark Twain said, "The two most important days of our lives are the day we are born and the day we find out why."

My co-author learned this lesson in a significant emotional experience that forever changed his life. In Dan's words:

One day during my American football practice session, the coach whistled, 'go,' and another player and I ran full speed into each other to practice our tackling technique. After a brutal head-on collision where my helmet crashed into his helmet and my shoulder was smashed into the cutting edge of my fiberglass pads, I lay on the ground in shock, with a sharp, piercing pain shooting through my body. My eye drooped and my speech slurred (which momentarily returned). I had compressed my vertebra in my neck, severed the axillary nerve in my right deltoid, and suffered a grade-2 concussion.

By nightfall my neck was stiff and swollen, my right side was numb, my arm dangled by my side, and I perspired profusely, shook, and threw up until I cried myself to sleep. For the next fourteen months I was paralyzed—both physically and emotionally. My heart was broken, my dreams were shattered, my identify was stolen, and my successful and promising life came crashing down.

Now that I've recovered, I'm often asked what took so long? Simply: I kept asking the wrong questions. I was asking the doctors how to get better when I should have been asking myself, 'Why?' As soon as I answered the *why* and felt the *want*, figuring out the *what* and *how* was simple. Once I stopped focusing on having fame and chasing fortune and started focusing on achieving my real purpose and becoming whole, I was able to persevere the pain of rehabilitation and do the hard things required to become everything I was really born to be.

THE BIOLOGY OF THE BRAIN

Make no mistake. Dan didn't recover from his paralysis because some motivational speaker gave him a raw-raw speech on 'you can if you think you can!' There was real science behind it. And the good news is that everybody who has been physically injured or emotionally wounded can also recover for the same reasons.

After hearing Dan's story I was intrigued enough to research how what he learned can help all of us. Bottom line: the human brain is divided into two major parts: the 'why' we do what we do and our 'wanting' to do it exist in the Limbic part of the brain that controls our feelings and decision making. The 'what to do' and 'how to do it' exist in the Neo-cortex part of the brain that controls our rational thought and language.

Notice that the decision-making (why) and feeling (want) function of the brain reside in a completely different place than the rational thought (what) and language (how) function of the brain. This is why it is oftentimes difficult to explain why you do something simply because it *feels right*.

A clearly defined *why* coupled with a compelling *want* (goal) have a gigantic impact on behavior because they engage more than simply the brain. They also engage the heart. Research proves that a clear, concise, personally meaningful and challenging goal causes our blood to pump more rapidly, our brain to fire, and our muscles to engage.

When we have only a *what* and a *how* without a *why* and a *want*, no such effects take place.

Clarity Identifies Your 'Why'

Dan concluded this interview with the following instruction: "Clarity begins when you realize there is a difference between the person and the performance – that failure is an event, not a person. It turns out that I couldn't begin to recover from my injury until I acknowledged that playing football was just what I did, not who I am as a man. And when you confuse who you are with what you do, and identify yourself in terms of what you do instead of who you are, you become a 'human doing' instead of a 'human being,' unacceptable if significance is what you seek.

Because adversity is what introduces us to our 'real' selves, I am the man I am and have the perspective that I have because of my devastating football ordeal. Yes it broke my heart and shattered my dreams, but through it all, I found a Clarity in life that has forever changed the way I face my fears and deal with pain. I now know:

'I always win. Either I win or I learn.'

'Pain is a signal to grow, not to suffer.
Once we learn the lesson the pain
is teaching us, the pain goes away.
In life there are no mistakes, only lessons.'

'Real motivation comes through getting clear on your 'why'
because you can't motivate yourself and inspire others with just
what you do. You must be able to articulate why you exist and
the purpose of every task you are asked to perform. Clarity on
your 'why' is the source of your ambition and the emotional
fuel that drives you to want to succeed and reach your ultimate
capacity and potential as a human being – not because it's
expected by others, but because it's demanded of yourself!'

Character Awareness

Clarity Reveals Your 'Who'

So... who are you – really? When no one is around? When you are alone with your thoughts and dreams and goals?

We human beings naturally and instinctively fight to survive, not to succumb. The human spirit is the most powerful force in the universe and is controlled by our inherent ability to face our fears and struggle, if necessary, to make it through life's storms. For this reason, our personal value and self-worth should always be the sum total of our thoughts, not the result of a miscalculation and multiplying of our insecurities.

Of all the illustrations I could pick there is none better than the story about when King Louis XVI of France was forced from his throne and imprisoned, his young son, the prince, was taken by those who dethroned the king. They thought that if they could morally destroy the king's son, inasmuch as he was heir to the throne, he would never realize the great and grand destiny that life had bestowed upon him.

They took the prince to a community far away, where they exposed the lad to every filthy and vile thing life could offer. They exposed him to foods that would quickly make him a slave to appetite; they constantly used vulgar language around him; they surrounded him with lewd and lustful men and women; they exposed him to dishonor and distrust. He was surrounded twenty-four hours a day by everything that could drag the soul of a man as low as he could slip.

The prince faced this treatment for more than six months, but not once did he buckle under pressure. Finally, the men questioned him. Why had he not submitted himself to these things. Why had he not partaken? These things—there for the asking—were desirable and would provide pleasure and satisfy his lusts. With a special sense of self, the boy humbly answered, "I cannot do what you ask, for I was born to be a king."

How does this answer and personal belief effect you? Do you believe this about yourself? I recently visited a girl friend who had a baby. As I walked to her hospital room to deliver the flowers and a congratulations card I walked past the nursery. When I looked through the window and saw the twelve tiny beautiful babies lying there in their little beds it occurred to me that every one of them from every different race was born to succeed. Every one of them laughed and cried for the same reasons. Every one of them needed to be held and cuddled and loved. Every one of them would grow up with dreams.

As I left the nursery to find my friend it dawned on me that although each of these babies was starting out in the birthing center with exactly the same attitude, as she and he grew up would they all stay positive and remain the same? Will some of them forget they were born to be kings and queens?

Behavioral scientists, psychologists, and social anthropologists who study human interaction teach that our sense of self affects our relationships more than anything else and is the quality that attracts others to follow us.

> *Do you compare yourself against others or against yourself? In the frightening world of anorexia and bulimia, commonly called "eating disorders," the ironic reality is that neither one of these conditions has anything to do with food. If you put a young woman on a deserted island with no access to fashion magazines flaunting the photo-shopped pictures of society's version of a beauty queen, and there were no other people around to compare her self with, would she be tall or short, smart or dumb, fast or slow, large boned or petite, ugly or pretty, fat or thin? Says who? Compared to what?*
>
> *Do you know that you are beautiful and handsome and magnificent just the way you are?*

CLARITY UPDATES YOUR 'WHAT'

As you now realize, when your 'why' does not jive with your 'what' it can cause a contradiction that leads to pain and disappointment. For example, a family friend is a beautiful, intelligent twenty-year-old young woman who is an extraordinarily successful songwriter in Nashville. Consequently, the lead singing "bad boys of the band" are attracted to her, and she was falling captive to their celebrity attention. To some fathers, this is no big deal. However, her caring and conservative dad, knowing the probable collateral damage of such fast and furious friendships, continually counseled her to make sure she knows the end result is tied to the beginning choice.

To his dismay, his fatherly advice fell on deaf ears, and his precious daughter continued to date the 'wild prima donnas' until her dad spoke from an epiphany he had experienced. He compared his daughter to a dog chasing cars. If the dog caught the car, what would she do with it? Just let it drag her down a road she had not intended, with a high probability that she would end up as a broken soul on the side of the road of life?

Although she got what she thought she wanted at the moment, would she really want what she got? In this "aha moment," his daughter changed her probable future by seeing through a different lens and making a wisely informed choice. Because her core values and the way she had been raised were different than those of the 'reckless men' she was dating, it was only a matter of time before they had a falling out.

Clarity may be about plotting and planning how to get what you think you want at the moment. But character based Clarity is about making sure you do what is necessary so you will want what you get. It's true: When the things you deeply believe in and think about are different than the things you do, you will never be happy.

The Six Steps To Finding Clarity

Obedience

We must realize we are not born into this world with a noble character. Instead, we are given our 'freewill agency' to choose our thoughts and their accompanying actions, which means our character is not developed in the great moments of test and trial. That is only when it is displayed.

Character is formed and fashioned in the workshop of our daily lives, during the uneventful, commonplace routine of life, when and where we struggle to take control of our thoughts and actions. Character is acquired, strengthened, and sustained by continuous practice. Proverbs 22:6 reads, "Train up a child in the way he should go, and when he is old, he will not depart from it."

For this reason, character is always linked to obedience. Your obedience builds your character, and your character will be showcased through your obedience. The way you live outweighs any words you may profess to follow.

Attitude

The most important thing about attitude is that we control it at all times, in all places, for every reason! No one can make us feel any way than how we choose to feel. When your "attitude" is right, your ability will always catch up!

According to Dan, those who wonder "Is the glass half empty or half full?" have missed the point. It's refillable! Thinking positively or thinking negatively does not fill up the glass. The pouring does! It's easier to act your way into positive thinking than to think your way into positive action. It's not the sugar that makes the tea sweet, it's the stirring – it's the process." This means attitude is not a noun - it's an action verb! In this mindset the old adage is true: Happiness is not found in the destination, but in the journey.

To find attitudinal Clarity:

Make a list of things that make you happy
Make a list of things you do every day
Compare the lists
Adjust accordingly

TRUST

It is nearly impossible to have a meaningful relationship with someone in whom you have no trust. Character development is accelerated when you can trust and rely on someone, more than you trust and rely on your own resources, strengths, and intellect, knowing that the person will protect you from anything that would cause you harm or destruction, and always reward you for your right choices and good works.

Growing up my parents reminded me and my siblings, to "always be loyal to those who are not present." Which means, that if we are talking with some friends and one of the people in our conversation gossips, saying something unkind, accusatory, or untrue, about someone who is not in the conversation, as soon as we leave each other, every one of us is going to wonder what that person is going to say about us individually, when we are not around.

GRATITUDE

When you have an obedient, positive, trusting heart, you have a thankful heart full of genuine appreciation for those who care enough about you to look out for your best interests. A "grateful heart" is a heart that genuinely and deeply appreciates someone's goodness. It is difficult to find a thankful rebellious person. One of the first things that open the door to rebellion in our hearts is being ungrateful.

HUMILITY

Being humble doesn't mean you are quiet, soft-spoken, self-deprecating, unassuming, less fortunate, or poor. Authentic "humility" entails being teachable and submissive – surrendering to the authority or control of another and yielding your self to the will of a higher power.

Growing up my family loved to ride horses. One of my most vivid memories was watching a trainer get an 'unbroken' horse to take a saddle, bridle and bit. Having been to some horse races I now know that when training Secretariat, the greatest thoroughbred racehorse of all time, his handlers didn't break his spirit. They broke him only to the point of submissiveness so that his talent and energy could be bridled and guided to help him reach his full potential. When we're humble, we retain a strong affection for others, concern ourselves with their welfare, and find ourselves unselfishly devoted to something larger than ourselves.

Reflection

In Michael Jackson's song 'Man In The Mirror,' he reminds us that the ultimate step in finding and maintaining Clarity is actually self-reflection and personal resolve:

> *I'm gonna make a change, for once in my life*
> *It's gonna feel real good, gonna make a difference*
> *Gonna make it right*
>
> *That's why I want you to know*
> *I'm starting with the man in the mirror*
> *I'm asking him to change his ways*
> *And no message could have been any clearer*
> *If you wanna make the world a better place*
> *Take a look at yourself, and then make a change.*

A favorite illustration of this is the story of the mother who came home from work one afternoon with an unfinished project she had to complete before returning the next day. As she laid the papers out on the kitchen table, her young daughter ran to meet her, pleading for her to spend some time playing. Knowing it would take her two hours to finish, mom scrambled to create a distraction that would allow her time to work.

Thankfully there was a magazine on the counter with a picture of the world on the front cover. Immediately mom ripped off the cover, tore it up into small pieces, put it on a piece of cardboard, and excitedly told her daughter it was a puzzle. With a smile, mom explained that as soon as her daughter was able to complete the puzzle, they would play until bedtime.

Her daughter left the room, and mom got to work. But to her surprise, just fifteen minutes later, her little girl was back, and the puzzle was assembled. Amazed, her mother asked how she finished so quickly. Her answer was, and is still the most significant step in finding and maintaining Clarity. "It was easy," she said. "On the other side of the picture of the world was a picture of a woman. When I got the woman right, the world was right!"

DISCUSSION QUESTIONS
CHAPTER 1: CLARITY

1. What does "when the things we deeply believe in and think about are different than the things we do, we will never be happy" mean to you?
2. What makes you happy?
3. If someone described you to someone else, what would they say?
4. What does Obedience mean to you?
5. What does it mean to have a positive Attitude?
6. What does Trust mean to you?
7. What does Gratitude Mean to you?
8. What is Humility?
9. How would you evaluate your sense of self, and current "man/woman in the mirror?"
Positively Strong / Negatively Weak
10. How would others rate your self-esteem?
Positive / Negative

Character Challenge

I challenge you to memorize (and firmly believe) the following statement of personal truth, so you can recite it every night before you go to sleep:

Clark Credo

*"I'm smart, talented, and I never say never.
I'm wanted, important, loveable,
capable, and I can succeed.
I love music and get good grades in school.
If I get knocked down or fall,
I just get back up and go again.
I never say 'I can't' – I always say 'I can, I will.'
If I spill or make a mistake, I just clean it up,
learn why, and say 'no big deal.'
I treat others how I want to be treated
so when people leave me they always say,
'I like me best when I'm with you – I want to see you again.'
I am on planet earth right now for a specific reason—
so unique and special that my DNA and fingerprints are
mine and mine alone. I will therefore be the very best
version of me, for I will make a lousy somebody else!"*

Chapter Two

CHARACTER

HONESTY

What happens to a person when they choose to tell a lie
When caught up in the moment – you can see it in their eye
An eye twitch to the right reveals a shift inside their mind
For when you tell a lie, you have to think of your next line

When you tell the truth – and your story does unfold
You won't need to remember when, or whom you just have told
So let's be honest now and keep it real without a spoof
And know the value of your words, when you just tell the truth.
(Copyright Alexandrea Sims 2017)

HONESTY IS A word that is simply incontestable. Everything in life is either true or false. There is no such thing as a "grey area," and nothing can ever be "half-true." In fact, there are no two sides to every story. There is only one complete "truth."

I have been taught from an early age that it's much better not to know than to have answers that are wrong. You can have understanding without knowledge, but having knowledge without understanding is worthless. Understanding our knowledge is the why to taking action.

We should never believe everything that we think. For example, we all know what happened in our country on September 11, 2001. Thirteen fanatical religionists hijacked four planes that they tragically crashed into the World Trade Center Towers in New York City, into the Pentagon in Washington, D.C., and into a field in Summerset, Pennsylvania when they attacked America.

For thirty days after this horrific event, our youngest most impressionable children, ages 12 and under (6th graders and below,) were caught in a constant state of paranoia. Loud noises scared them; full of fear and trembling they could not concentrate. Consequently, the School Counselors across America took it upon themselves to conduct a nationwide survey to determine what was causing this immobilizing fear. The survey was only one question long, which simply asked each child to describe what happened. Astonishingly, every child explained that bad men stole some jets and crashed them into buildings, killing thousands of people, and "they kept doing it."

Because every television in every school faculty lounge, library, restaurant, store window, and home was tuned into the news 24/7, these innocent, vulnerable, most impressionable children could not differentiate between live T.V. and video replay. So, they believed we had been attacked ten to twelve times, every day for thirty days in a row! No wonder they were afraid! No, we should never believe everything that we think.

Seeking "Whole Truth"

This makes honesty, (which absolutely must be "whole truth,") the most important character trait, attribute, and essential quality to possess. In fact, without total honesty, no other character trait really matters at all. In the business world, the definition of sales is "the transference of trust." And because each of us is constantly "selling" our personalities, priorities, and prejudices to each other in hopes we can become friends and associates, every one of us needs to accept and embrace this definition and "transfer trust" in everything we say and do.

Yes, trust and truth are synonymous with honesty, and according to author Mark Twain, they are the secrets to simplifying our lives: "If you tell the truth, you don't have to remember anything."

Honesty Is Having "Integrity"

Obviously, being totally honest and always telling the truth means we choose to live a life of "Integrity." Author Dr. Spencer Johnson said, "Integrity is telling myself the truth. And honesty is telling the truth to other people. We must not be afraid to stand up for what is right, no matter how tough the situation." Integrity means being the same at home, at school, at play – the same on the field, as we are off the field – the same off stage, as we are on stage – the same honest, responsible person doing the right thing when people are watching, but more importantly, doing the right thing when people aren't watching.

To illustrate: Dan was once taking a five-hour flight from California to Florida. He was sitting in first class and eventually got up to use the lavatory in that section of the plane. He entered the tiny room, locked the door, and was immediately blindsided by a gross, putrid, gooey, mystery muck snaking its way down the mirror, with used paper towels on the sink, dirty water splashed from corner to corner, and repulsive "residue" on the slimy floor.

When he stopped gagging, it occurred to Dan that the person who came in right after him would think that he did all this! Ha! So he held his nose, cleaned it up, and finished his washroom break.

However, before he returned to his seat, Dan stood and stared into the faces of the other twenty-three first-class passengers, silently asking, "Okay, which one of you low-budget slobs trashed this washroom?"

Now in his seat, starring out the window to gain his composure, Dan realized an important life lesson: You cannot buy class – and class certainly entails the exercise of total honesty and integrity. What a shame, and a disgrace, that so many think money and power make them somebody they are not!

Are we not all guilty of getting on Facebook and Instagram and "twisting" our current reality into a fabricated fantasy that we are prettier, smarter and more talented than we really are, and that our lives are cooler and better than others?

Integrity Is Facing The Brutal Facts Of Reality

Psychologists, personal development gurus and our teachers continuously tell us to "be present in the moment." But what if your "present reality" is brutal, uncomfortable, painful, and depressing? The answer is that you strive to live in your more pleasant past or in a more hopeful fabricated future, or seek to numb your current circumstances with alcohol, drugs or prescription medication.

Can you relate? I can. So the question is: what are we supposed to do about it? How can we change our mindset and perception so it changes our reality? Dr. Wayne Dyer said, "When you change the way you look at things, the things you look at change."

The solution to this debilitating predicament begins when we acknowledge that part of our life experience on this earth includes some time in the "wilderness." The good news is that we don't go "into" the wilderness – we only go "through" it. Yes it is scary to walk into the unknown where it may get dark and dreary, and we may trip on a fallen branch or stumble on the bumpy trail and fall. But while we are in this wilderness surrounded by giant trees, the experience becomes transformational because of two evident truths:

> *"Happiness is like a tree going up into the sky, and sadness is like the roots going down into the womb*

of the earth. Sadness gives depth - happiness gives height. Sadness gives roots - Happiness gives branches. The higher a tree goes and the bigger it grows, the bigger and deeper the roots. Both are needed for balance - simultaneous and in proportion."

"A bird sitting on a tree is never afraid of the branch breaking, because her trust is not in the strength of the branch but in her wings and ability to fly."

THE WILDERNESS

Great quotes, but the practical application is manifested only when you willingly 'Face the Brutal Facts of Reality and embrace each wilderness experience. Let me explain:

Throughout history, it seems that all great leaders have had a wilderness experience - a significant emotional event away from life as they know it, where they have to ask tough questions and discover who they are, why they are, and what matters most to them during a time of self-reflection when they focus and finely tune their thoughts and cleanse their souls.

Only those who fail, fall, sacrifice, and go without are humble and contrite enough to learn the deepest, most meaningful lessons: that when we hit a wall or make a mistake, we always look at it as a wilderness experience - not as an end but as a new beginning; not as a closed door but as an open door.

U.S. President Abraham Lincoln's string of failures is documented and much talked about. U.S. President Franklin D. Roosevelt flunked out of Columbia Law School because he wasn't smart enough. Basketball superstar Michael Jordan was cut from his high school basketball team as a fifteen-year-old kid because he wasn't good enough.

Mahatma

As an attorney in the courtrooms in India, Mahatma Gandhi presented a terrible image of himself. He was too frightened to stand up to his opposition and was easily overwhelmed.

As he reached his lowest, most wretched level of suffering and realized that he would never become a prominent attorney, he took his outward challenges and turned them into an inward wilderness experience that took him from India to South Africa, where he spent twenty years as an expatriate in nonviolent resistance to England.

In the moments of suffering during his worst failures, Gandhi looked at himself, didn't like what he saw, saw others more down and out than he, and developed his own passive nonresistance philosophy that led him back to his native India to lead his people to independence from British rule.

Mickey?

One day inside a cold, damp garage in the Midwestern United States a struggling, half-starved illustrator was sitting in his 'wilderness,' exerting his brain for inspiration, when a mouse ran across his foot. Generally speaking, mice smell up a place, are not welcome, make a nuisance of them selves, and are afraid of humans. Not this one! This mouse boldly strutted across the floor and into the hole in the wall.

"The mouse doesn't even respect me," he thought. "Why should I respect myself?" But it was at this lowest, most humble point, that he began to imagine what that confident, pesky, perky mouse was like, and he began to draw and develop its personality. America and the world have never been the same since that unknown mouse, who was quickly named Mickey, had a chance encounter with the discouraged, unknown illustrator named Walt Disney.

14 Super Successful People Who Finatically Failed At First

WINSTON CHURCHILL failed the sixth grade. He was defeated in every public office role he ran for. Then he became the British prime minister at the age of 62.

THOMAS EDISON's teachers told him he was "too stupid to learn anything." Edison also famously invented 1,000 light bulbs before creating one that worked.

HARLAND SANDERS, the famous Kentucky Fried Chicken "Colonel," couldn't sell his chicken. More than 1,000 restaurants rejected him. Finally one said yes, and today there are thousands of KFC restaurants bearing his image all over the world.

STEVEN SPIELBERG was rejected from his dream school, the University of Southern California, three times. He sought out an education somewhere else and dropped out to be a director.

MARILYN MONROE's first contract with Columbia Pictures expired because they told her she wasn't pretty or talented enough to be an actress.

ALBERT EINSTEIN didn't speak until age four and didn't read until age seven. His teachers labeled him "slow" and "mentally handicapped." But Einstein just had a different way of thinking. He later won the Nobel prize in physics.

SIR ISAAC NEWTON was tasked with running the family farm but was a miserable failure. Newton was sent off to Cambridge University and became a physics scholar.

The first time JERRY SEINFELD went onstage, he was booed away by the jeering crowd. Eventually, he became a famous comic with one of the most-loved sitcoms ever.

OPRAH WINFREY was fired from her television reporting job because they told her she wasn't fit to be on screen. But Winfrey rebounded and became the undisputed queen of television talk shows. She's also a billionaire.

HENRY FORD's first auto company went out of business. He abandoned a second because of a fight and a third went downhill because of declining sales. He went on to become one of the greatest American entrepreneurs ever.

DR. SEUSS' first book was rejected by 27 different publishers. He's now the most popular children's book author ever.

J.K. ROWLING was unemployed, divorced and raising a daughter on social security while writing the first Harry Potter novel. J.K. Rowling is now internationally renowned for her 7 book Harry Potter series and is the first person to become a billionaire from writing.

VINCENT VAN GOGH only sold one painting in his entire life, to a friend. He sometimes starved in order to create the 800 paintings he'd eventually do. Today, his works are priceless.

VERA WANG failed to make the U.S. Olympic figure-skating team. Then she became an editor at Vogue and was passed over for the editor-in-chief position. She began designing wedding gowns at 40 and today is the premier designer in the business, with a multi-billion dollar industry.

Going into your wilderness is not an experience of failure but rather a moment of truth, a wake-up call experience of refinement that takes you to a place you cannot take yourself - a place not occupied by what happens to you but by the lessons you are learning and by what you are doing with what happens to you. Let us never forget that the best way out of anything is through it.

Honest Integrity In Science

From a scientific perspective, our brains connect to experiences. The significant moments in our lives tend to stick with us for long periods of time because neurons in our brains never divide or die off, and new ones do not replace them. The core component of our nervous system is the neuron, and it determines which memories become stored, and which ones are not. The vivid memories that stick with us are the moments that have an impact on our lives, and these memories helped shape us into the people that we are today. Those moments were significant experiences and will always be remembered.

In contrast, when we lie, we can rarely remember every single detail that we mentioned in our tall tale? When we lie, science shows that our eyes will look up and to the right, insinuating that your brain is "visually constructing images or sounds" that it has never actually seen or heard. Usually, when the person is telling the truth, they will look to the left because they are accessing the part of their brain that is "visually or auditory remembered" – meaning that this person has actually seen or heard what they are about to tell you.

So, why is it so hard to be honest in this day and age? Unfortunately, we see this all around us in our schools, neighborhoods and country where we are bombarded with "fake news" from the media and from our politicians and others whom we are supposed to be able to trust.

Confirmation Bias

It is critical that every one of us is aware of a communication phenomenon social scientists call "Confirmation Bias." Under confirmation bias, we seek out and assign more weight to evidence confirming our personal hypothesis and ignore or don't fully consider evidence negating someone else's hypothesis.

In public discussions, confirmation bias plagues us by saddling us with self-fulfilling social, political, and racial prejudices. Investigators and journalists often perpetuate confirmation bias by framing data in ways that confirm their views and personal conclusions, as in the case of television news programs where the producer chooses "expert guests" based on whether the guests share the producer's political and social biases.

Is this not a mockery of our sacred and cherished freedom of the press?

You can get right, correct, truthful, negative answers if you ask negative questions and go down a negative path; and you can get right, correct, truthful, positive answers if you ask positive questions and go down a positive path.

By asking only certain kinds of questions, we allow ourselves to ignore inconvenient facts or accept mere speculation as fact. Such tendentious questioning can yield information that proves just about anything to our own satisfaction and enables us to get what we want.

The good news is that most reputable journalists – those who have strong and unshakable Character - make conscious efforts to avoid confirmation bias! Do you? Do I? Is it too much to expect that every decision maker should be held to this high standard of 'Whole Truth Honesty," total integrity and communication excellence?

Being Authentically Real

Bottom line: We need to make three commitments to our selves. First, we must commit to being "present" and alert in every moment. Which means we will willingly enter our 'wildernesses,' face the brutal facts of our reality, and will do more than hear, we listen. We do more than listen – we first "seek to understand – will to be understood." Most importantly, we allow ourselves to feel, which allows us to be completely honest with ourselves regardless of what is being said to us or happening around us.

Ask yourself, "Are you completely present in each moment? Or do you text while talking to someone else? Or take a call on your cell in the middle of a conversation? Or…?

The second part of being "present" and fully engaged in every moment is to honestly identify the times we are not fully engaged because we are distracted by our phones and computers. Honestly evaluate yourself: Which of the following eleven distractions are altering your focus, diminishing your concentration on the task at hand, holding you back, and dragging you down? Procrastination? Social Media Surfing?

Interruptions? Constantly Responding To Facebook Posts, Snap Chats, Insta Posts and E-mails? Multi-tasking? Taking Home Calls At Work? Taking Work Calls At Home? Non-productive Appointments? Socializing and Gossiping? Disruptive T.V.? Viewing Inappropriate Internet Sites? Texting Someone Rather Than Calling Someone? (And the worst,) Personal Posts That Ruin Your Reputation?

The third and final part of being "present" and fully engaged in every moment is to commit to honestly explaining exactly what happened at that moment. The facts are the facts – the truth is the truth. It's not about who's right, but what's right. Russian Novelist Fyodor Dostoyevsky said, "Above all, don't lie to yourself. The man who lies to himself and listens to his own lie comes to a point that he cannot distinguish the truth within him, or around him, and so loses all respect for himself and for others. And, having no respect, he ceases to love."

Hmm, could this mean that before you can like someone else, you must first like yourself? Before you can truly love someone else, you must first love yourself? Before you can fully trust someone else, you must first fully trust yourself? Only when you are totally honest can you expect others to be totally honest with you? Honesty is a one-way street, so go down that road with confidence, and you will never have anything to question.

Honoring Promises

One of my favorite illustrations is the story of a young Japanese boy who was spending the weekend with his elderly grandfather. The rendezvous would take place at the train station, for the grandfather lived in a village on the other side of the mountain. The boy's parents dropped him off, hugged both of them good-bye, and drove away.

As the two of them waited in line to buy their tickets, the grandfather discovered that he had left his wallet on the previous train. He didn't have any money. It was cold and as the wind picked up he asked the ticket lady if she would loan him yen valuing fifty dollars. The grandfather promised he would pay her back later that night.

Because of the Japanese culture's deep and abiding respect for its elders, the ticket lady believed the grandfather and paid for their tickets. An hour later, they arrived in the village. They walked fifteen minutes through the horrible weather and finally entered the cottage. Hungry, tired, and soaking wet, the grandfather went to his drawer and retrieved some money. "Let's go," he said.

His grandson rebutted, "But Grandfather, I'm starving, and we're going back to the train station in three days. Why can't you just pay her back then? It will cost you the price of two more round-trip tickets to go now, just to pay back two one-way passes." Putting on a dry overcoat, and handing his grandson a wool blanket for comfort, the eighty-year-old grandfather put his arm around his grandson's shoulders and taught him the lesson of the ages. "Son, we must get there tonight before the counter closes and she goes home. This is not about money this is about honor. I gave her my word, and we must always keep our promises!"

Character Challenge

How will you practice honesty today? Identify something you have said this week that may not have been 100% true, and first ask yourself why you felt the need to change facts or add details? Then reconfigure that story back into a 100% true statement. Really ask yourself before you speak, "Is what I'm about to say the whole truth and nothing but the truth?" Challenge yourself to practice honesty every day.

DISCUSSION QUESTIONS
Chapter 2: Honesty

1. What does "transference of trust" look like to you?
2. What can you do or say when others are being unkind to someone who is not there?
3. What does Mark Twain mean when he says, "If you tell the truth, you don't have to remember anything"?
4. Is there harm in presenting yourself in a better way on social media? How does that hurt us? How does it hurt others?
5. Is it possible to help others during their wilderness?
6. What "wilderness" have you experienced?
7. Why do people lie?
8. Is honesty difficult? Why or Why not?
9. How does social media influence honesty?
10. How does staying positive influence our relationships?
11. What does it mean to be "in the present"?
12. How does technology take us out of the present?
13. Why is it important to be honest every day?
14. Is there harm in a little white lie?
15. How do you feel when you find someone has lied to you?
16. If you don't say anything, are you being honest?
17. Who is it most important to be honest with – others or yourself?

Chapter Three

Character

Anti-Bullying

What is your first thought when a kid's alone at school
Maybe he's in trouble, or perhaps he broke a rule
But what if, what we don't know is some kids were being mean
His heart was broken; he was bullied, all behind the scenes

If no one else is with you when you witness harmful deeds
You could turn your back, or help another who's in need
So, if you see a friend or foe get picked on for a fight
Be a strong example and stick up for what is right.
(Copyright Alexandrea Sims 2017)

Webster's dictionary defines **Bullying** as: "A person who uses strength or power to harm or intimidate those who are weaker – typically to force him or her to do what one wants." Synonyms include oppressor, tyrant, tormentor, and persecutor.

Psychiatrists and therapists all agree that everyone (male, female, old, young, of any race, color, or creed,) who puts somebody else down, either physically, mentally, emotionally or socially, do so because they are insecure.

Most likely, their lives are *not* going as they think they should, so they wake up each day with the "victim mentality," of "whoa me, life isn't fair." Research shows that feelings of inadequacy and anger in children, often originate from an adult in that child's life maintaining a negative outlook on their own miserable existence. The child's inadequacy and anger develop as the adult takes it out on the child. Obviously, we repeat what we see and hear, and this verbal, emotional, and often times physical abuse of the son or daughter manifests itself in the child when he/she leaves home. This is the way they have been raised, and therefore this is how they interact with others outside the home.

In a tongue-in-cheek, yet serious illustration, why do people watch "Jerry Springer" on television? Because, no matter how bad and disfunctional their lives are, "at least their lives are not as pitiful, or as complicated, as the fools on T.V.!"

Bottom line: Whenever we feel stagnant and believe we are stuck in a rut of no return, which means we have stopped dreaming and working hard to achieve a good, clean, pure, powerful, positive, productive goal, our natural tendency is to put someone else down to make us feel like we are making progress. We default to a "comparative analysis" looking for others who are easy targets to attack mentally, emotionally, and physically, because they are weaker and less fortunate than we are. And in our insecurity and lack of direction and motivation we somehow think by putting them down we are better than we really are!

Remedy Solution

Everyone who is bullying someone else simply needs to realize the positive transforming power of dreaming a mighty dream. If you don't have a dream, how are you ever going to make a dream come true? In life, we can't wish it were easier. We need to want to get stronger, smarter, and better. It's been said, "When you lose your dreams, you die." That's why we have so many people walking the halls of life who are dead, and they don't even know it. Those who bully have died before they're dead, and only a dream that stirs hope in the future with a clearly defined purpose for living will resurrect them.

Then why is "Bullying" a national crisis and why has it become such a huge challenge at home, in school, and at play? According to the National Bullying Prevention Center, more than one out of every five students reported being bullied in 2016. Bullying is defined as: "Unwanted, aggressive behavior among school aged children that involves a real or perceived power imbalance. The behavior is repeated, or has the potential to be repeated, over time."

Bullying includes actions, such as making threats, spreading rumors, attacking someone physically or verbally, and excluding someone from a group on purpose. This definition alone doesn't even begin to describe the impact this issue has on our youth. As we already mentioned, there are four major ways in which the insecure engage in Bullying: Physical bullying, Verbal bullying, Social bullying, and Cyber bullying. The reasons for being bullied reported most often by students are: Appearance (Looks) (55%), Body Shape (37%), and Race (16%.)

The "Cyber bullying" among teens has sky rocketed in the last two years. In 2014, NoBullying.com provided the statistic that (52%) of teens reported being cyber bullied, and in 2016 Teen Safe Inc. statistics show that (87%) of teens reported instances of cyber bullying. I believe the high demand for social media in the past two years has had a huge impact on these percentages.

Hundreds of kids are being allowed to participate in online interactions without parental supervision. Peer pressure has been an issue for years now, so add social media into the mix, and it gives kids, even more opportunity to bully without getting caught. It is easy for kids to hide behind a computer screen without consequences, because parents may be unaware of their children's actions. Parents should have full access to all of their children's social media accounts to make sure that they are using them in a positive way.

Although "Bullying" is a subject that is often discussed, it is difficult to resolve in school by the administration, teachers, or counselors, because most of the time it is done outside of the school or classroom setting. This is why Character Awareness includes this significant Anti-Bullying message that is a crucial topic we should discuss with our youth and their parents. Becoming more aware of bullying, whether you are the bully or the victim, is the first step in turning this problem into a challenge that all of us can embrace and solve together.

What Can Each Of Us Do – Right Now – Today?

The first thing each of us needs to do is Stop using the word "Bullying." Why? The subconscious mind cannot differentiate between real and imagined. Therefore, every time we are told *not* to do something before we can "not do it," we must first create a visual image in our mind of "doing it."

For example, when we tell someone, "Don't spill the milk," he must first create a visual image of spilling the milk before he can comprehend what it means and what it looks like to "not spill it." Because our thoughts create our behavior, this mindset makes us more vulnerable and apt to spill the milk, than to not spill it. For this reason, let us replace the negative word and accusation of being a "Bully" with the positive word and visualization of being a "Friend."

In sports, such as American football, coaches make a horrible mistake when they make their players watch the film of their previous game, and continually rewind, and show a player doing something wrong – taking a wrong first step, getting too high on the block, not tackling properly, running the wrong way, etc. Reinforcing, and reminding the player how "not to do it correctly" burns the unacceptable behavior into his psyche, as both a mind and muscle memory. Significant coaches, teachers, counselors, parents, and friends catch one another doing something right, and focus on the positive alternative to a negative word or hurtful action.

Our Many Roles – "Bully" or "Friend"

There are many different roles that children can play. They may be bullied, they may bully others, they might witness bullying, or decide to prevent bullying and stand up for what is right. In every case, the way we change and strengthen our resolve is to simply ask how we want to be treated? Then we simply start treating others in the manner we wish to be treated. Obviously, everybody wants a "best friend." But to have a best friend, we must first be a best friend, and a best friend is "someone who brings out the best in us."

When children treat others as less important than themselves, we must ask the hard question. "Why?" What makes certain kids feel like they are better than another child? In these "crucial conversations," we need to address the issue we have already introduced, and blatantly ask the Bully, "Does putting someone else down really make you feel better about yourself?"

And if by chance he agrees, because he too has been the victim of being continuously put down, then the solution to helping him change his negative attitude and hurtful behavior is to use the proven process called the "ABC Observation Model."

Proven Solution
"A-B-C Observation Sequence"

I learned this 'ABC Model' from my sister who is a Middle School Special Education teacher with an emphasis on the severely challenged. Although all educators are wonderful, when it comes to changing someone's attitude and undesirable behavior, I personally believe that my sister and her amazing colleagues are the most qualified experts in the world.

I have been in her classroom and have witnessed how this process works. It is sometimes referred to as S-R-S or the Stimulus-Response-Stimulus.

- The "A" stands for the antecedents, or what triggers the behavior.
- The "B" stands for the actual behavior that results from the antecedent triggers.
- The "C" stands for the consequences of the behavior.

In order to change someone's unwanted disobedient behavior into desired obedient behavior; you have to figure out the motivation behind their behavior. This motivation could be one of three things:

- To gain attention or gain something tangible.
- To avoid or escape.
- To receive sensory stimulation.

By determining the function of the behavior, you can then select a "target replacement behavior," that serves the same function and an intervention plan that will allow the child to turn inappropriate behaviors into appropriate behaviors.

Do What?

What Goes Around Comes Back Around

A unique directive was initiated at a high school in northern Utah, where students with a physical or mental challenge were fully integrated into the mainstream classes and curriculum. To make it work, the administration organized a mentor program that teamed up one special-needs student with a mainstream student who would help him or her along.

Character Awareness

The athletic director presented the idea to the captain of the football team. John was a tall, strong, intense young man—not the patient, caring type needed for this kind of program. He made it clear that this "wasn't his thing" and he didn't have time to be a mentor. But the athletic director knew it would be good for him and insisted that John volunteer.

John was matched up with Randy—a young man with Down syndrome whom a few of the insecure guys in school teased and bullied. Reluctant and irritated at first, John literally tried to "lose" Randy, but soon John welcomed the constant company. Randy not only attended every one of John's classes and ate with him at lunch time, he also went to football practice. After a few days, John asked the coach to make Randy the official manager responsible for the balls, tape, and water bottles.

At the end of the football season, the team won the state championship, and John was awarded with a gold medal as the Most Valuable Player in the state. Randy was presented with a school letterman jacket. The team cheered as Randy put it on. It was the coolest thing that had ever happened to him; from that day forward, Randy never took it off. He slept in his jacket and wore it throughout each weekend.

Basketball season started, and John was also the captain and star of that team. At John's request, Randy was again named the manager. During the basketball season, they were still inseparable. Not only did John take Randy to special occasions— like dances as a joint escort for his girlfriend—but he also took Randy to the library to tutor him in his classes. As he tutored Randy, John became a much better student and made the honor roll for the first time in more than a year.

The mentor program was unveiling itself as the most rewarding year of John's life. Then tragedy struck in the middle of the state basketball tournament. Randy caught a virus and suddenly died of pneumonia. The funeral was held the day before the final championship game. John was asked to be one of the speakers. In his talk, John shared his thoughts about his deep, abiding friendship and respect for Randy. He told how Randy had been the one who had taught him about real courage, self-esteem, unconditional love, and the importance of giving 100 percent in everything he did. John dedicated the upcoming state finals game to Randy and concluded his remarks by stating that he was honored to have received the MVP award in football and the Leadership Plaque for being the captain of the basketball team. "But," John added, "the real leader of both the football and basketball teams was Randy, for he accomplished more with what he had than anyone I've ever met. Randy inspired all who knew him."

John walked from behind the podium, took off the irreplaceable, twenty-four carat- gold state football MVP medallion that hung around his neck, leaned into the open casket, and placed it on Randy's chest. He placed his captain's plaque next to it.

Randy was buried in his letterman jacket, surrounded by John's cherished awards, as well as pictures and letters left by others who admired him. But this is not the end. The next day, John's team won the championship and presented the game ball to Randy's family. John went to college on a full athletic scholarship and graduated with a master's degree in education. Today John is a special education teacher and volunteers ten hours a week for the Special Olympics.

"Purpose?"

Dan was speaking to members of Our Primary Purpose (OPP), a highly acclaimed program for chemically dependent teenagers in Des Moines, Iowa. At the third meeting, just for parents, a mother whose son was not enrolled in the OPP Program, shared her story:

Her twenty-year-old son, John is handsome and talented, a good citizen, a good student, a good musician, and a gifted athlete. He also had a lovely girlfriend and seemed to have no problems. One day, he stopped talking as much as he usually did. Thirty days passed, and his conversation dwindled to nothing. He was depressed, and his parents and girlfriend continually told him that they loved him. He knew that they loved him, and he expressed his love for them. Everyone was concerned about his well being and wondered what they could say, or do to help him, since saying "I love you," obviously wasn't enough to improve the situation.

Character Awareness

John finally made a move. He locked himself in the cellar. Although he was down in the dim dampness for three days without food, he continued to acknowledge his parents' love for him, and his love for them. But his depression deepened, and his loved ones were convinced suicide was imminent. Healthcare professionals were brought in, but the counseling, kindness, caring, and love did not help.

On the third day of John's isolation, the local high school football coach (who didn't know what was going on in John's life) called his home to talk to him. John's mother said, John was busy and took a message at the coach's request. Then she went to the cellar door and called down the stairs, "John, Coach Ivers just phoned."

He said that his players voted last night on who they want their assistant coach to be. They said you were the greatest Pop Warner football coach they had ever had, and now they think they can win the state championship if you help coach them. Coach Ivers said they need you. He needs you! He said, "If you're interested, you should be at football practice at 2:45 p.m. this afternoon."

Do you know what happened? Sure you do! John came out of the cellar and went to practice. He accepted the coaching job, and by the time he came home from his first practice, he had snapped out of his depression. He once again felt needed, wanted, and important, and he was back to his old self again.

Question: How does this illustrative experience apply to solving the Bullying challenge in our families and schools? The answer should be obvious. When we feel good about ourselves because we are actively engaged in doing something positive to prove to ourselves that we are "needed," we automatically stop trying to put somebody else down, because we are so busy reaching out to lift others up.

Character Challenge

Do you know anyone at school who is currently getting picked on, or do you engage in "bullying" yourself? It is important to be aware of what is going on around you, as well as, the impact your actions are having on others. Today, watch for someone being bullied and immediately identify how it makes you feel to see someone being beat down physically, mentally, emotionally and/or socially, just to make the insecure person (who is doing the bullying) feel stronger or more powerfully important. With this newly acquired empathetic understanding, I challenge you to stick up for the next person you see being bullied and remember that the simple and powerful solution is to be his/her friend. Helping others by sticking up for what's right will have a positive impact on your character, and on the life of the new friend, you helped during their time of need.

DISCUSSION QUESTIONS
Chapter 3: Anti-Bullying

1. What does bullying look like at your school?

2. How would you stop cyber-bullying if you were an adult?

3. How can you tell others to "stop bullying" with a positive mindset?

4. What changes do you need to make to be a "best friend"?

5. What does Jason mean when he says his school counselor listens?

6. How can you listen better to friends, teachers and family members?

7. How would better listening affect your relationships?

Chapter Four

Character

Responsibility

What's your first reaction when you spill onto the floor
Do you walk away, or do you clean up what you poured
The choice is yours, but your reactions speak for themselves
Will you take full ownership, or blame it on "the elves"

We make new choices daily, and your fate is in your hands
To do your best, and not complain when things don't go as planned
So why not start today, and be proud of who you are
And take responsibility, it's time to "raise your bar."
(Copyright Alexandrea Sims 2017)

Responsibility has many different synonyms and definitions. Webster's dictionary defines it as: "The state or fact of having a duty to deal with something or of having control over someone." Authority, Importance, Liability, Obligation are synonyms or other ways of saying it, but what does it really mean? When you think about "the act of being responsible," what first comes to mind?

Taking responsibility doesn't only mean owning your actions, but it also implies being accountable for your thoughts, your feelings, and your wishes. It questions your character and makes you look deep within to evaluate your life choices. There are those who say they are going to do something, and those who actually follow through and accomplish those things. People that "walk the walk," instead of just "talking the talk."

There's a theory of mine that I like to call the "Dope List." When we complete tasks that have been racking up our "To-do" lists, a small amount of Dopamine is released in the brain. Dopamine is a chemical produced in the dopaminergic neurons in the Ventral Tegmental Area (VTA,) and is commonly associated with the "pleasure system" of the brain. When we finally get that shot of dopamine for completing a certain task, also known as a "reward seeking behavior," it makes us feel good, and therefore want to complete more tasks to be able to feel good again.

We should not only be setting goals daily, but we should be writing them down, so that when we complete them and physically get to check something off that list, we get that unmatched feeling of accomplishment that makes us strive to be more productive. Taking responsibility is truly so much more than just being responsible. It is about creating healthy habits that will make us want to continue down that "Dope List" path, get our daily shot of Dopamine by using our time wisely and taking responsibility for accomplishing the goals in our lives. Sigmund Freud once said, "Most people do not really want freedom, because freedom involves responsibility, and most people are frightened of responsibility."

Blaming And Complaining

Imagine yourself as a therapist, and a young woman comes into your office and starts to yell and cry and whine that the reason her life is out of control is because of her father; that her dear old dad is the cause of her pain and misery.

What council would you give her? Would you suggest bringing in her father so you could begin treating him? It is only logical that if he is the cause of her woes, if you cure him, her pain should go away? Have you ever experienced a similar situation?

Taking full responsibility for your every thought and action means you must **release all thoughts of blaming**.

Do you ever enjoy a brisk rampage of blame on the government, or the terrorists, or the Chinese, or the oil companies for high gas prices, or McDonalds for our obesity?

When you stop and refine your thinking to take 100% responsibility, you realize that you're either participating in creating that situation or allowing it to continue.

Taking responsibility for your life also requires that you **release all your complaining**. What have you recently complained about?

In order to complain, you've got to have a reference point of something you want; an item or a situation that is better than what you have now or more desirable than what someone else has - something you have not been willing to risk creating. So you feel entitled to complain about it instead. Perhaps you have been complaining about your job; that would mean that you believe a better job than the one you have exists somewhere out there.

What is it? Where is it? What are you doing about it?

When someone is complaining about something it means they know there is something they can do about it, because people don't usually complain about the things they cannot change.

The ironic truth is that complainers usually whine and voice their complaints to those who can't do anything about the issues.

Think of one thing you most often complain about. To help you stop complaining, ask yourself:

What would I rather have? Why do I want it? What will it cost me in time and resources to get it? Am I really willing to pay the price now so I can enjoy the prize forever? Will I actually want it when I get it? What is my first step to getting it?"

Personal Experience

In my professional dance career, personal responsibility is one of the most important things I have had to learn to accomplish. I moved to Los Angeles to pursue my career when I was 18 years old. Feeling terrified for what was to come, but knowing I couldn't wait to make my dreams of becoming a professional dancer come true. Day after day, I relentlessly worked on my craft, taking countless amounts of classes, going to every audition I was invited into, then waking up and doing it all over again. I was truly taking responsibility for my future and putting everything I had in to making my dance career a reality.

Within my first six months, I booked my first World Tour with Latin Superstar, **Chayanne**. The other seven dancers on this tour were all over the age of twenty-six and had been working in Los Angles for many years prior to this tour. I was eighteen years old at the time, and it was one of my first big jobs. I was terrified, but being "thrown into the bull pin," made me rise to the occasion.

During the process of preparation for the tour, I made sure that I was the first one to rehearsal, and the last one to leave. I went to the gym, on top of rehearsing for 8 hours a day, to make sure I was always at the top of my game. When the tour rolled around, I developed the habits of always being prompt for my show call time, and never late for the bus in the morning. I took pride in my health and stamina performing to the best of my ability every single night.

Along with responsibility comes discipline. Business philosopher Jim Rohn said, "Discipline is the bridge between goals and accomplishment." It's not just about being told what to do and doing it, but it's about taking it upon yourself to go the extra mile to accomplish all of your goals.

My hard work did not go unnoticed, and I was hired again for Chayanne's next tour that took place one year later. Why do you think they brought me back for a second time? With all do respect to myself, and to others in my same profession, there are hundreds of dancers in Los Angeles qualified enough to go on tour. Yet, I was still asked to return. Why do you think that is? Because they knew that they could count on me.

DEPENDABILITY

So, what also comes with "Responsibility" and "Discipline?" "Dependability." If people know that they can depend on you, then they will always want to be around you. This is how you develop trust in all relationships in your life, whether they are business or personal.

Responsibility has nothing to do with age, race, color, or creed; it is all about how much pride you take in your character, and your ability to make things happen for yourself.

Former British Prime Minister, Winston S. Churchill said, "To each there comes in their lifetime a special moment when they are figuratively tapped on the shoulder and offered the chance to do a very special thing, unique to them and fitted to their talents. What a tragedy if that moment finds them unprepared or unqualified for that which could have been their finest hour."

In other words, the price of greatness is to take personal responsibility for your time by always giving maximum effort in every situation so you will be 'lucky' enough to accomplish many extraordinary things. Remember, the definition of luck is when preparation comes face to face with opportunity. If you want to be great, you must take responsibility for your actions and actively pursue your dreams until they are no longer your dreams, but they are your reality.

Essayist Anais Nin once said, "What we call our destiny is truly our character, and that character can be altered. The knowledge that we are responsible for our actions and attitudes does not need to be discouraging because it also means that we are free to change this destiny. One is not in bound to the past, which has shaped our feelings, regarding race, from inheritance, or background. All this can be altered if we have the courage to examine how it has formed us. We can alter the chemistry, provided we have the courage to dissect the elements."

Accepting More Responsibility

In a different sense, the word Responsibility is always good. The first half of the word – "Response," means "taking best appropriate action to a thought or situation." By nature, however, it is still a reaction and fluctuates between "will you" or "won't you." The second part of Responsibility – "Ability," never fluctuates because it's always about if you "can" or "can't."

And if you can, you must lead, give more, serve more, do more, be more, take it to the ultimate level, consistently winning and gaining what you want. Why? Says who? It is an actual written law of the universe: "where much is given, much is expected," which means that regardless of our age or interests, we can get anything in life that we want when we are willing to help enough other people get what they want. In other words, taking responsibility is deciding to give more than we take – to help ourselves by helping others!

It is this "service before self," mindset that we understand why and how responsibility is recognizing the relationship between pain and gain, payment and prize. We all have heard, "No Pain, No Gain," which in the attitude of "Responsibility" means, "No Heart, No Chance," translating into being willing to pay the price every day, so you have earned the right to enjoy the gained prize forever. "Responsibility" is making the right choice based on that recognition and then living with the choice without concern.

In sports, responsibility means that every coach and player on the team "makes winning personal." In life, it means we make self-discipline and doing the right thing a personal choice – not because leaders do expect it, but because it is demanded of ourselves!

Responsibility Breeds Leaders

The ironic and exciting thing about taking personal responsibility for our thoughts and actions, rewards and consequences of our choices, is that we automatically become leaders. Why? Because we automatically become more empathetic to the mistakes of others, realizing we are human – they are human – and we all need to cut each other some slack and support one another in every good, clean, pure, powerful, positive, productive way as we are all doing our best to accomplish personal goals.

Because we humans are "herd animals" and social beings, we are attracted to people like us and naturally form groups based on interests, job assignments at work, athletic teams, and clicks at school to create support. School administrators, counselors, teachers, coaches, parents, friends (you and I) all are part of a click, and each one of our clicks has a leader (with or without a title) who emerges based on respect, integrity, work ethic, and communication skills.

For this reason, let us conclude this discussion by raising our "Awareness" from society's claim that leaders are responsible, period – to the authentic, realistic understanding that "yes," the buck must stop somewhere and it is ultimately at the top. But every one of us must also and equally participate in that responsibility and do everything in our circle of power, skill set, and influence to help the leaders accomplish what he/she and the group/team needs to accomplish.

A parent, coach, school administrator, teacher, leader, manager, and/or good, conscientious, *caring friend is only responsible to people, not for them.* We cannot improve others; rather, we can only inspire them to change their minds, objectives, goals, vision, and clarity of cause, so they want to improve themselves. Remember, we can't coach results, we can only coach behavior, and inspired people don't have to be motivated! When your "Why?" is bigger than your "Why not?" and your "Why?" is your own, taking personal responsibility for your thoughts, actions, victories, defeats, successes, and failures becomes authentically automatic.

Bottom line: We must constantly remind those whom we lead that they cannot merely think their way to a new way of living. They must live their way to a new way of thinking. This obviously applies to ourselves, as all outcomes in our existence will be determined by the values, attributes, and traits we choose to live by.

After four thousand years of recorded history, the two most difficult things we have to deal with are failure and success – both of which are internal issues we are responsible for. Therefore, don't let your destiny fall short. Let us all take responsibility for our lives today, and be the person we were meant to be.

CHARACTER CHALLENGE

Think of something you've talked about doing in the future, and go out and do it today. Write out what that task is, and after you've completed it, write how it made you feel to finally complete the task and accomplish that goal? If you continue to actively take responsibility for your time, your life will become more productive, and you will finally have control of your own destiny.

DISCUSSION QUESTIONS
Chapter 4: Responsibility

1. What responsibilities do you have at home? At school?
2. What does personal responsibility look like at your school?
3. Who is responsibility for making sure your homework gets done?
4. Who cares more about your grades – you or your parents?
5. Who is a leader at your school? What makes people want to follow them?

Chapter Five

Character

Addiction Prevention

Addiction is a challenge many people suffer from
It isn't something that is very easily overcome
For if it gets ahold of you, it ruins every day
But if you catch it early, you can choose to walk away

Drinks and drugs are everywhere in media and sight
Once these things consume you, then you can't put up a fight
But if we never try them we won't break our family's hearts.
It's easy to say no if you just choose to never start
(Copyright Alexandrea Sims 2017)

ADDICTION IS DEFINED in a few different ways. As an adjective, it means: "Devoted or given up to something psychologically, physiologically, and physically habit forming." As a noun, it means:

"A person who is addicted to a particular thing, activity, habit, or substance." As a verb, it means: "To habituate or abandon oneself obsessively and compulsively to become dependent on something."

Many people associate the word addiction only with drugs and alcohol, but the definition of addiction is more far reaching than this including sex, pornography, the Internet, and even use of our cell phones. For these reasons, we must become Aware of the many ways in which "addiction" manifests itself in our lives, and fortify actions to protect us from its horrible short term, and long term effects.

Stereotypical Addiction

The National Center on Addiction and Substance Abuse states, "Addiction is a complex disease of the brain and body that involves compulsive use of one or more substances despite serious health and social consequences." It affects millions of people all over the world, and the problem is only getting worse. Families have torn apart; loved ones have been lost to this dangerous world of abusive substances, and many people can't escape. Isn't it interesting though, that we can literally become addicted to anything, even an activity?

I have never had a drug or an alcohol problem, but I have suffered from an addiction with the last word mentioned above: "Activity." There was a time in my life where I was so addicted to exercise that it was extremely detrimental to my health. You'd never think exercise could be a bad thing right? Wrong. I would run on an elliptical for up to three hours a day. No matter if I had to wake up at 4 a.m. to get on an airplane, I would still manage to get myself to the gym to run. I know some of you are thinking exercise is good for you.

However, too much of anything isn't healthy. It is a dangerous form of addiction for many people and is very hard to overcome. Luckily, I overcame my addiction with the help of many friends along the way. I am here to tell you it wasn't easy. It takes a lot of discipline to get out of such a negative headspace, and everyone needs some support to do it. Moderation in all things is something we should all strive for.

If you ever find yourself feeling like you can't function throughout your day without it – it's time to get some help. If you, (or a loved one) are struggling with addiction, it is never too late to seek some help. Even just discussing it out loud, with a trusted person in your life, can do wonders for your wellbeing.

I have a friend, Spencer, whose family has torn apart because his mother was addicted to alcohol, as well as prescription drugs. It caused a massive problem for his family, and eventually completely tore the family apart when he was only sixteen-years-old. He is now thirty-three, and his mother, still to this day, is suffering from the same terrifying addiction behavior. After being through many treatment sessions, and rehabilitation centers, she still has yet to overcome her addictions, even after seventeen long years.

As I spoke with Spencer about how it has effected his life, he mentioned to me that he always wonders what his life would have been like if his mother had never started using drugs and alcohol in the first place. Would his parents still be together? Would he have a relationship with his brother, whom he hasn't spoken to for the last eight years because his brother couldn't stand trying to help his poor mother, who doesn't seem to want to be helped in the first place?

The worst part of this story is that Spencer is in no way alone with his situation. Thousands of American families have been torn apart each year from these same issues, and it breaks my heart to hear story after story with the same outcome.

Mind-Chemical Addiction

The human brain manufactures, secretes, and releases four major chemicals to accomplish four different results, for four different reasons. They are:

- Endorphin: the pain-masking chemical
- Dopamine: the goal achieving chemical

- Serotonin: the leadership chemical
- Oxytocin: the chemical of love

These four chemicals can be divided into two separate categories – "Selfish" and "Selfless."

- Selfish chemicals – Endorphin and Dopamine help us endure and get things done and achieve more.
- Selfless chemicals – Serotonin and Oxytocin strengthen our social bonds create meaningful connections and collaboration.

Research shows that we can become "addicted" to two of these chemicals!

Endorphins are pain-masking chemicals that help us push ourselves through tough circumstances. Scientists tell us they are more powerful and more addictive than morphine. It is the famous "Runner's High" when athletes who love to run every morning or work out hard in the gym, do so because they are literally "addicted" to the euphoric feeling caused by endorphins.

Dopamine is the most dangerous chemical of the four because it is the most satisfying. Alcohol, nicotine, cocaine, and even cell phones send dopamine through our body whenever we use them, which is what makes those things so highly addictive. Even completing tasks, achieving goals, and simply getting things done can give us a rush of dopamine. That's why crossing items off of your "To-do" list feels so great.

Cellphone Addiction?

Since dopamine makes us feel great, we instinctively do things that give us a quick dopamine fix without considering the value of those things. Most frequently created, and released when we use our cell phones. Dopamine is what produces that irresistible urge to check every notification on your phone. Each time we clear the notification, respond to the text, or read an email, it gives us a boost in dopamine.

If you take your phone to class, then to dinner, and to the washroom, you are addicted to your phone. If the first thing you do every morning when you awaken is look at your phone, you are addicted. If you are driving and hear the "ping" that you just received a text, or an email, or a "snap chat," and you absolutely have to look at it right then, you are addicted to your phone!

In a speech delivered in October 2017, world renowned youth leader Bonnie Oscarson gracefully pricks everybody's conscience with an obvious observation:

"We live in a culture where more and more we are focused on the small little screen in our hands than on the people around us. We have substituted texting and tweeting for actually looking someone in the eye and smiling, or even rarer, having a face-to-face conversation. We are often more concerned about how many followers and 'Likes' we have than putting an arm around a friend and showing love, concern and tangible interest. As amazing as modern technology is for staying connected to family and friends, it has become a poor and ineffective way to actually communicate."

There is no way to emotionally convey and connect heart to heart, spirit to spirit and soul to soul with anyone about anything through emails, texts, tweets, and the rest of our typed out social media messaging. Experts teach us that communication is 70 percent non-verbal where gestures, body language and especially eye contact are the most important and significant ingredients in meaningful conversations. If we are not vigilant in choosing a better way to use our personal devices, it is only a matter of time before we turn inward and fall victim to the fact that in order to develop real and meaningful relationships we must interact at the sensory level engaging all of our senses of sight, smell, hearing, tasting and human touch.

We are touched when we see the great needs of those who are suffering around the world, but because we are distracted and addicted to our cell phones, we may fail to see a lonely person sitting next to us in class who needs our friendship.

Research shows that when someone texts while driving, on average they take their eyes off the road for only five seconds at a time. However, a car traveling 60 miles per hour travels the length of a football field (100 yards) in five seconds. It only takes one or two seconds to veer into the oncoming lane of traffic, and hit someone head-on, and kill them, their family, our friends or selves. Let us never forget that the #1 cause of automobile accidents and teenage deaths – is "distracted driving" – because they are addicted to their phones and can't wait 10 to 30 minutes to finally pull over and safely respond to a message!

In real life, no one wants to be a "slave" to anyone or anything. A prison will collapse when the inmates start running it. The tail can never wag the dog. I challenge all of us to stop letting our phones "run" our lives!

Pornography Addiction

Research suggests that looking at pornographic materials, both printed and in video/movies, desensitizes a man's feelings of respect and compassionate admiration towards a woman while dehumanizing her inward and outward beauty to that of a lusted after "object" of desire. Therefore, it is critical to point out the powerfully negative influence that pornography has on our personal and professional relationships – especially on our teenage boys trying to figure out how to be a man.

Yes, we can find statistics that back up the assumptions that pornography is harmful, but we can also flash statistics that backup the other side of the discussion, suggesting pornography has little or no effect on our minds, hearts, habits, and behavior. My opinion? If there is even a slight possibility that it could desensitize your emotions and ruin your most intimate relationship, why take that chance?

To illustrate, Dan was flying cross-country with his daughter who was ten-years-old at the time. They were playing cards. In the middle of the game, he asked her to hold her cards up closer to her face, so he could not see them. She turned to him scowling and said, "Just don't look!"

Any questions? Am I going to fast? Will you accept my challenge to "stop it" and choose to walk on "higher ground?" What every woman and every man really want is one who has not been negatively influenced by television, and desensitized by pornography, or the Internet; who let themselves truly feel and engage all of their senses in every moment.

Real Solution To All Addictions

"Service Before Self"

World renown motivational teacher Zig Ziglar taught, "You can get anything in life that you want when you are willing to help enough other people get what they want."

As a young woman, even with my limited experience as a twenty-four year old, I have discovered this to be absolutely true! The quickest way to find our selves is to lose ourselves in the service of others. Service transforms the servant and the served. Whoever renders service to many puts him/her self in line for greatness – great wealth, great return, great satisfaction, great reputation, and great love. Rabindranath Tagore reported, "I slept and dreamt that life was joy. I awoke and saw that life was service. I acted and behold; service was joy."

For seventy-five years, **Alcoholics Anonymous** has taught the world the one true and simple secret to mental and physical health, wealth, enduring happiness, and how to achieve the level beyond success. It is found in the 12-Step Program, which has helped millions of people free themselves from their addictions, get on the road to recovery, and stay on the journey of significance by adhering to important truths.

Beginning with Step 1, which is to admit you have a personal problem, the participants embrace one step at a time, one day at a time, until they've experienced the healing and helping power in each step.

However, everyone who is involved at any level in "AA" knows that even if they learn, believe, embrace, and follow all of the first eleven steps, unless they engage in and fully embrace the twelfth step they will start drinking again. The only way they can beat their addiction and truly heal from this disease is through the one simple secret found in Step 12: Serve and help another addict overcome addiction and volunteer in the community.

Bottom line: To recover from any hard thing, heartache, broken dream, ruined relationship, lost job, loss of a loved one, or addiction, the secret lies in realizing what goes around, comes around. Through service, both the giver's life and the receiver's life are changed, stretched, and transformed for good. For this reason, we all should rise to the occasion to:

Serve In Five Special Ways

Serve just to serve – when and where others won't.

Serve out of duty, honor, and gratitude.

Serve your school and affiliate organizations in a way that allows others to accomplish more with you than without you.

Serve a cause larger than yourself.

Serve someone who can't repay you.

Because our addictions "flat-line" our emotions, which causes a numb reaction and alienated response to our most important relationships with those who love us the most, recovery is difficult. Frequently, the rocky road that eventually led us to our addiction usually began when we did something wrong, harmful or inappropriate, and something occurred that made us feel deeply remorseful, shameful, and full of guilt. In order to begin the full recovery process, we must first face the brutal facts of reality with a willingness to forgive.

Research shows that most addictions begin when we don't know how to cope with what just happened, and it perpetuates itself because we have never taken the time to "forgive" ourselves and let go of the guilt we are experiencing. This, in turn, prohibits our ability to "forgive" others and get on with our lives addiction free. For this reason, it is important for you to feel the messages found in this true story. Although it is unrelated to addiction, it illustrates this most important point:

ETHICAL FORGIVENESS

A strict disciplinarian stood in front of our class with a crew-cut hairstyle and piercing eyes. He had been a marine drill sergeant in the Vietnam War, had his master's degree in psychology, and was welcoming us as the professor of Business Ethics. Rumor had it that this macho man tolerated nothing. He explained as part of the course orientation that he could always tell if someone cheated.

Sarcastically, he illustrated, "One time I called a young man on the carpet. I accused him of cheating. He promised, 'No, I didn't.' I countered, 'Yes, you did.' 'No, I didn't.' 'Yes, you did.' 'How did you know?' He finally confessed. I answered him, 'The young lady you were sitting next to wrote on her test paper, 'Don't know the answer.' You wrote, 'Me neither!' "

We all laughed at his story but took it to mean that if anyone got caught cheating, he would "rip their lips off" and flunk them out of school. The weeks passed uneventfully until the day of the midterm. A guy on the third row was caught cheating. Everyone held his or her breath as he was asked to leave and turn his exam in early. Surely, he would be kicked out of the university. To our surprise, the young man was back in class the next Monday. One indignant student finally raised his hand to interrupt the lecture. "Mr. Jacobsen, Professor, sir. I think this is totally absurd. Here you are teaching a class on ethics. You catch a student red-handed, cheating, and you don't suspend him. What kind of a lesson are you teaching us?"

The professor smiled and replied, "Great question, and I'll answer it with a story." He told the class the story of a certain one-room schoolhouse in the mountains of California that no teacher could handle. It was a school just for boys, so rough that the teachers would resign after only a few short days. A young, inexperienced teacher applied, and the old director warned him about the out-of-control, disrespectful students. The teacher took the job anyway.

On the first day of school, the new teacher greeted them, "Good morning, boys. I'm here because I care about you." They yelled, "Yeah, right. You don't even know us," and they laughed and made fun at the top of their voices. The teacher continued, "Now I want to run a good school, but I confess that I do not know how unless you help me. The things we help create, we support. Suppose we have a few rules. You tell me, and I'll write them on the chalkboard."

One fellow yelled, "No stealing." Another yelled, "On time." Finally, ten rules appeared. "Now," said the teacher, "A law is not good unless there is a consequence attached. What shall we do with one who breaks them?"

Big Jake yelled out, "Beat him across the back ten times without his coat on." The teacher replied, "That is pretty severe, boys. Are you sure that you are ready to stand by it?" They all yelled, "Yeah, yeah, beat them to death." The teacher said, "Alright, we will live by them. Class, come to order."

Two weeks later, Big Jake, the toughest of the tough, found that his lunch had been stolen. Upon inquiry, the thief was located – a little hungry fellow, ten-years-old. "We have found the thief, and he must be punished according to your rule – ten stripes across the back. Vincent, come up here," the teacher ordered.

The frail little boy, trembling, came up slowly with a big coat fastened up to his neck and pleaded, "Teacher, you can lick me as hard as you like, but please, don't take my coat off."

"Take the coat off," the teacher reminded. "You helped make the rules." As he began to unbutton, the little guy had no shirt on and revealed his bony little-crippled body. "How can I whip this child?" the teacher thought. But, I must do what I say I will do if I'm going to keep control and respect of the others. "How come you are not wearing a shirt, Vincent?" the teacher asked.

"My father died, and my mother is very poor," he replied. "I have only one shirt to my name, and she is washing it today, and I wore my brother's big coat to keep me warm."

The teacher, with a rod in hand, hesitated and then reluctantly asked Vincent to turn around. Just then Big Jake jumped to his feet and interrupted, "Teacher, if you don't object, I will take Vincent's whipping for him." Hiding his disbelief, the teacher thought quickly on his feet, "Very well, there is a certain law that one can become a substitute for another."

Off came Big Jake's coat, and after five hard strokes, the rod broke. The teacher bowed his head in his hands and thought, "How can I finish this awful task?" Then he heard the class of macho men sniffling and sobbing. What did he see when he lifted his head? Little Vincent had reached up and caught Big Jake with both arms around his neck.

"Jake, I'm sorry I stole your lunch, but it had been two days since I had anything to eat. I was extra hungrier than usual. It was just sitting there with no one around, and I didn't think. Jake, I will love you until I die for taking my beating for me. I will never steal again. Yes, you are my hero!"

The college professor stopped talking. There wasn't a dry eye in the room. With tears streaming down his cheeks, he said to our class, "My name is Vincent Jacobsen. I was that frail, crippled, hungry lad. We all will make mistakes at some point in our lives, and sometimes all we need is just one break to get our lives back on track. This course is on ethics, and if you remember nothing else, remember that forgiveness is a powerful part of ethical behavior. Thanks for your inspirational example Big Jake, wherever you are."

Character Challenge

Think of something in your life that you feel as though you depend on (besides physician prescribed medication,) whether it be coffee, soda, exercise, alcohol, etc. I challenge you to say "no" to this thing for one full day. Wait a few days, and go without it again. Begin to train your brain that this substance/activity is not necessary for your life or well-being. Write down how it made you feel to be able to say "no." Express to yourself how empowering it feels to be in control of your thoughts, choices, and behaviors. Remember, Character development begins when we know we are in charge of our destiny and can change the direction we are heading on a moments notice. Make today your first step to freedom.

Discussion Questions
Chapter 5: Addiction Prevention

1. How would you define addiction?
2. Why is it important to overcome addictions?
3. What "addictions" do you feel you have?
4. When does something you enjoy become an addiction?
5. How do you overcome addictions?
6. How have addictions affected your life?
7. Why is it important to have balance in your life?

Chapter Six

Character Consistency

*In life, we say to "fake it 'til you make it" while you climb
But what if you're authentic every day and every time
Cause when you act the same around your parents and your friends
You'll get a reputation that will back you 'til the end*

*It's important to decide just who you want to be
Then being that real person for the world to plainly see
Consistency is key in how we choose to spend our time
So let us always strive to be consistently sublime.*
(Copyright Alexandrea Sims 2017)

WEBSTER DEFINES **CONSISTENCY** as: "Steadfast adherence to the same principles, course, and form – agreement, harmony, compatibility, and uniformity among the parts of a complex thing."

Although the dictionary illuminates a positive outlook, there are some who view consistency as a negative character trait, quality and attribute.

George Bernard Shaw wrote: "Consistency is the enemy of enterprise, just as symmetry is the enemy of art." For those who have chosen a career that shackles them to a 9 to 5 routine, their view of consistency drastically differs from those who are self-employed, or part time in their field of work and don't necessarily work the same hours every week. It seems that Novelist and Writer, Aldous Huxley had them in mind when he said, "Consistency is contrary to nature, contrary to life. The only completely consistent people are the dead."

If you are someone who gets stuck in a routine and has a hard time getting out of it, staying in that particular state of being can be an extremely negative approach to life. As human beings, we are hardwired to want and need progress. If our day-to-day lives look the same week after week, it is no wonder why so many people hate their jobs – only look forward to Friday, instead of Monday – thinking they are paid by the hour, when in reality we are all paid for the value we bring to that hour. One of the character traits we value the most is consistency!

Isn't it obvious, that if we aren't pushing ourselves to our ultimate capacity and potential as a human being, someone else, somewhere else is? And when we meet them they will win! Doesn't the formula for creating enduring happiness include consistently moving forward, stretching our personal limits, pushing ourselves toward a higher goal, and constantly striving to become better today than we were yesterday? Consistently staying in a complacent state, stuck in our past and refusing to progress in every aspect of our lives is a very dangerous place in which to be.

Eric Hoffer said it best, "In times of change, learners inherit the earth, while the learned find themselves beautifully equipped in a world that no longer exists." For this reason, "Consistency" begins with the first step, realizing you don't have to see the top of the staircase before you start climbing the steps – finding value in only taking the next one. Consistency then turns into "Persistency," which drives us until we achieve our ultimate goal.

When we understand the true meaning of "Consistency," we realize success and significance are not achieved over night; and that "It's not the sugar that makes the tea sweet, it's the stirring" – happiness is not found in a destination, but in a consistent journey.

From The Entertainment World

Mega hit songwriter and Platinum Recording Artist, **Pharrell Williams** once said: "I am overly ambitious, because I realize it can be done." This is a man who has embodied the word "Consistency," and has created a successful life for himself through hard work and perseverance.

Being a professional dancer for most of my life, I have had many amazing opportunities to work with some of the greatest entertainers of all time. One of the remarkable musicians I have had the pleasure to work with is Mr. Pharrell Williams. In fact, I have worked with him on multiple occasions and have witnessed his greatness first hand. Not only is his career inspiring to me, but I admire the way he treats others in the public eye, it is the same way he appears to treat everyone he encounters. I have never before met such a gracious man who genuinely cares for others consistently.

I was one of twelve dancers on one particular project, and during one of our short breaks, Pharrell Williams took the time to ask me about my life, my family, and other hobbies that I enjoyed besides dancing. During that conversation, Pharrell Williams made me feel like he truly valued what I had to say.

Which brings me to my final point. We must be the same "off stage" as we are "on stage." No matter in what situation we put ourselves, we must always remain true to our character and treat others as we would like to be treated. As stated before, in business the definition of sales is "the transference of trust" which applies to all of us because each of us is engaged in relationship selling in every aspect of our lives.

Because we only do business with those whom we trust, and developing trust usually begins with a recommendation referral from someone else, it is critical to be consistent in everything we say and do. Our reputation depends on it!

Billionaire philanthropist Warren Buffett said, "It takes twenty years to build a reputation and five minutes to ruin it. If you think about that, you'll do things differently." Your reputation is simply how the rest of the world perceives you, and at the end of the day your reputation is all you have.

Being consistent is being predictable, where each part of you is congruent with every part of you, and there are no contradictions in your soul. Most likely you understand this and know it is the formula for being your authentic self. Sometimes you fall short of being "real" because you think your intentions make you consistently predictable and trustworthy.

Consistency Improves When We Understand The Interaction Between The Brain, Mind, Heart, And Body

Not so, because our bodies are the delivery system: Computer Brain, Thinking Mind, and Feeling Heart are only three of the four dimensions. We must acknowledge that our current reality is mostly revealed in our "Doing Action." Brain, Mind, Heart, and Body constitute the soul of man.

Stubbing our toe causes us to feel pain. Our toe hitting the table leg is a physical event and it causes our nerves to fire in a certain pattern, which sends a signal to our "Computer Brain." Which begs the question: Are mental states identical with physical states? Is pain just the firing of those neurons in the brain? If so, it would seem that our mind is nothing more than our brain. But if pain is something more than neurons firing, then there is room to conclude that our mind is something extra, something we have in addition to a body, a heart, and a brain.

Bottom line: The body experiences the pain, the brain feels the pain, but it is the mind that interprets the pain and decides how it will affect you. This means that it is not what happens to us, but what we do with what happens to us that defines who we are. In this context, the body and the brain are what happen to us and the mind is how we intentionally choose to either positively respond to what we value, or negatively react to the emotional weather around us.

Once we fully understand this, it is easy to realize that self is not discovered – self is created. Which is why some choose to be positive and continuously productive, and others remain their old, tired, stagnant, stale selves. Yes, they are consistent and predictable, but no one wants to be around a negative, complaining grump!

Obviously, creating self is a process that never ends because self-actualization and becoming consistently significant is an everlasting work in progress. To help us sustain our motivation to continually stretch and improve, we need to surround ourselves with others of like mind and who seek similar desired results.

As we can plainly see, Consistency is key in all things. It is necessary for personal progress, character growth, personality stability, and outlook on change. To truly become the person we want to be, we must constantly be striving for more and consistently overcoming any obstacle that is thrown in our way.

When you value your own personal character, approaching your life in a way that will benefit you and those around you, you will always be remembered for that. Everyone who meets you will have a positive, lasting impression. "In fiction, we find the predictable boring. In real life, we find the unpredictable terrifying and conclude it's better to have a predictable enemy than an unpredictable friend. This is why we can only be unpredictable once. Being predictable is synonymous with being consistent which is developed in the workshop of our daily lives, practiced in the uneventful commonplace routine of life, so in the great moments of test and trial our character can be displayed."

Be 'Unstoppable'

To conclude this discussion on the significance of being 'Consistent,' let me share another one of the pivotal events in Dan's fascinating life that illuminated his understanding of what it really takes to be 'Consistent' in thought, energy, focus, discipline, work ethic, and purpose. It began when Dan watched the final championship game in the NCAA Basketball Tournament way back in 1983 when coach Jimmy Valvano led his North Carolina State 'Wolfpack' to the National Championship. After fifteen years of coaching, Valvano became a popular television sports commentator. Tragically, he was stricken with cancer, and his long battle came to an end a few weeks after he delivered his final speech at the inaugural ESPY Awards (Excellence in Sports Performance Yearly Award) broadcast live on national television in 1993.

With tears in his eyes he pleaded: "Don't give up, don't ever give up."

Fast-forward to 2011 when Dan received a phone call from a young man who was being honored that year at the ESPYS. His name was Anthony Robles, born with only one leg, who had just gone undefeated and won the National NCAA Wrestling Championship. He was being honored as the recipient of the Jimmy Valvano ESPY Award for Perseverance and Courage, and he wanted Dan to help him write his acceptance speech.

Dan flew into Phoenix, Arizona and together they Googled Jimmy Valvano to get an idea of who he was, and why this prestigious award was named after him. The next few minutes would change both of their lives forever.

On July 13, 2011 Anthony walked out on stage on his crutches to a standing ovation from his fellow sports world superstars. With the world watching, he humbly honored his mother for never giving up on him even though she, a teenaged single mother, could have thought that raising a child with one leg was too much and could have given up Anthony for adoption. When Anthony was in college, and she became ill, and her husband walked out on the family and they lost their home – she still didn't give up.

Anthony's mother stretched to care for him and encouraged him to stretch to pursue his dreams of wrestling. Anthony recognized that not everyone understands the power of stretch: "At the beginning of my wrestling career, I lost most of my matches and people said, 'It's okay. I'm proud of you for trying.' This ticked me off so bad! Losing is not okay!"

"What they were really saying was that I was a handicapped kid and should be grateful that I could even participate." Following his mother's example, he refused to settle, stretched to achieve his goals, and has now dedicated his life to inspiring others to "stretch."

Anthony's story reveals that winning really is personal – and individual. While generic paths to success do exist (look at all the self-help books out there and the rules they expound,) everybody's own path to significance is by definition an outgrowth of who they are and what they were intended to be on this planet.

In measuring ourselves against ourselves, we should embrace our individuality and fearlessly verge into uncharted territory, even if others view us as quixotic, impractical, or crazy. To express this dedication, Anthony Robles closed his ESPY acceptance speech by quoting a short poem Dan penned for the occasion that captures the essence of what Coach Valvano represented, and what Anthony's inspirational story teaches the world.

UNSTOPPABLE

Every soul who comes to earth
With a leg or two at birth
Must wrestle his opponents knowing
It's not what is, it's what can be, that measures worth.
Make it hard, just make it possible
And through pain, I'll not complain
My spirit is unconquerable.
Fearless, I will face each foe
For I know, I am capable
Making winning personal

I don't care what's probable
Through blood, sweat, and tears
I am Unstoppable!
(Dan Clark ©2011)

CHARACTER CHALLENGE

It is now time for you to figure out how to apply "Consistency" to your own life. In the space below: Write the characteristics that you admire in someone else and find what areas you could work on. How will you "Consistently" improve your character today?

DISCUSSION QUESTIONS
CHAPTER 6: CONSISTENCY

1. What do you do consistently well?
2. Why is consistency and important character trait?
3. Who demonstrates consistency in your life?
4. Think of your favorite class. What would it be like if your teacher did not show consistency?
5. What things in school help you "stretch"?

Chapter Seven

Character

Thwarting Suicide

Do you feel alone, or like you don't have any friends
Do you feel there's no escape, this pain just has no end
Do you feel less than your peers, you see their life in lights
Do you think they have it made, they feel no pain or spite

It's time to reevaluate and look behind the scenes
And know you're not alone, this life's not always as it seems
Don't ever be too scared to talk, or open up by choice
You're needed, wanted, loved, and people want to hear your voice

You're stronger than you think and you can make it through this fight.
I promise there's a brighter day, beyond each darkest night!
(Copyright Alexandrea Sims 2017)

Webster's dictionary defines **Suicide** as: "Someone who deliberately and maliciously kills him/herself because he/she does not want to continue living; taking one's own life voluntarily and intentionally; a major public health challenge as well as a personal and family tragedy." **Thwarting Suicide** is to "oppose successfully; defeat the hopes or aspirations of; to prevent someone from doing something or to stop something from happening."

For this reason, we need to be aware of both sides of the discussion, explanation, and understanding of suicide. The hardline, somewhat cold-hearted discussion claims suicide is "the felonious act of self-murder," which is why some report that a person "committed suicide." If you believe killing oneself truly is murder, then "yes," and the person who took his/her life "committed" a crime. And, if you believe in a life here after, surely there will be a punishment that fits the crime.

However, as authors, it is our belief that no one ever "commits suicide." If they die as a result of hurting themselves, they have "completed" their suicide. In this way, we always honor the dignity and soul of every one of our fellow human beings who through some choices, relationships, and circumstances happened to get themselves in a dark place. By passing no judgment, or assigning no guilt, with a greater sense of empathetic understanding we acknowledge that we too, have been there. Only wishing we could have been with them at the critical moment to remind them that, "No matter what their past has been, they have a spotless future – hold on for one more day because 'in two more days, tomorrow is yesterday!'"

It is with this mindset that we illuminate our Awareness of Suicide, stating it is critical that we always remember there is a difference between the person and the performance. Failure is a momentary event, not a person. If you're not failing a few times, it means you are not pushing yourself hard enough. Sadly, it is the forgetting of this single mindset that leads someone to the downward spiraling conclusion that, "I am what I did, or what I am not doing."

I firmly believe that if we could somehow interview everyone who completed his/her suicide, each of them would tell us they would not take their lives if they had another chance. The reason why is revealed through hundreds of interviews with friends, and associates, who confess they have had "suicidal thoughts." At some point in their lives, they all agree that it was a simple shift from a negative destructive, "Whoa me, victim mentality" reactive mindset to a positive, proactive mindset that snapped them out of their frightening funk.

Alarming Statistics That Are Killing A Generation

The National Center for Injury Prevention reports that there were 41,149 suicides in 2013 in the United States – a rate of 12.6 per 100,000 is equal to 113 suicides each day, or one every 13 minutes. Males take their own lives at nearly four times the rate of females, and males represent 77.9% of all suicides, but females are more likely to have suicidal thoughts.

The rates as of 2015 have increased to a rate of 13.26 per 100,000, on an average of 121 per day. In 2015, adolescents and young adults aged 15 to 24 had a suicide rate of 12.5, which is the lowest rate among all other ages. There is one age group that caught my attention, the girls between the ages of 10 and 14. Though they make up a small portion of the total suicides, the rate in that group jumped the most – it experienced the largest percent increase, tripling over 15 years from 0.5 to 1.7 per 100,000 people.

Causes

Hopelessness and Lack of Human Connection

Research reveals that the two major reasons someone decides to hurt themselves are: "Hopelessness" and "Lack of Human Connection." This same research also shows that the five major reasons we slide into this emotionally distorted predicament are capsulized in the acronym H.A.L.T.S.: Hungry, Angry, Lonely, Tired and Sad. The longer we remain in any one of these debilitating situations, the weaker our resolve becomes to do what is necessary to escape. Before we realize it our desire, physical strength and energy to positively deal with what's happening has diminished to the point we choose not to deal and not to go on.

For these reasons, it is in everybody's best interest to become more "Aware" of how these symptoms are manifesting themselves in the pandemic completion of suicides in our neighborhoods, schools, communities, and country.

According to the American Academy of pediatrics, suicide is a complex act that represents the end result of a combination of factors in any individual. These factors include biological vulnerabilities, life history, present social circumstances, and the availability of means to complete it. While these factors do not "cause" suicide in the strict sense, some people are at greater risk of self-harm than others. Risk factors for suicide include: a family history of suicide; a history of abuse in childhood; a local cluster of recent suicides or a local landmark associated with suicides such as the Golden Gate Bridge in San Francisco; recent stressful events such as failing to make a team or win a scholarship, parental separation or divorce, upsetting medical diagnosis, and the death of a family member or friend; the presence and easy access of firearms in the house; and alcohol or substance abuse because mood-altering substances weaken a person's impulse control.

Attention/Media Coverage

Media should never give out detailed descriptions of the method used in a suicide to avoid possible duplication. The media also must be very careful to not give any glorification to a victim and should in no way imply that the suicide gave them any sort of media attention. Not everyone contemplating suicide is seeking attention, but for those that are, any sort of media attention whatsoever could possibly provoke them to act out in a dangerous manner.

Shedding light on suicide can be a tricky thing to do, because of something called "Contagion," which means the communication of disease by direct or indirect contact. The Department of Health and Human Services mentions that direct and indirect exposure to suicidal behavior has been shown to precede an increase in suicidal behavior in persons at risk for suicide, especially in adolescents and young adults.

Survivors Of Suicide

One group of people that is often overlooked in discussions of suicide is the friends and family left behind by the suicide. It is estimated that each person who kills him/herself leaves six survivors to deal with the aftermath; thus there are at least 4.5 million survivors of suicide in the United States. In addition to the grief that ordinarily accompanies death, survivors of suicide often struggle with feelings of guilt and shame as well. They often benefit from group or individual psychotherapy in order to work through such issues as wondering whether they could have prevented the suicide or whether they are likely to commit suicide themselves. The American Foundation for Suicide Prevention (AFSP) has a number of online resources available for survivors of suicide.

More Than "Cliché"

At the risk of coming across as a "rah-rah" motivational speaker, and rather than waiting until the end of this discussion to present some solid solution, let's conclude this chapter discussion by listing the Four Fundamental Truths that everyone whom we interviewed admitted were at the heart, mind, and soul of positively altering their lives forever.

Four Absolute Realities

1. WHEN YOU CHANGE THE WAY YOU SEE THINGS, THE THINGS YOU SEE CHANGE.

You can't coach results – you can only coach behavior. Behavior is created 100% by what you think and your perception of what you see. When you change the way you see things, the things you see change.

Example: A father promised his son that if he practiced all day, he'd play baseball with him after work. The father arrived home, and they went into the backyard.

"Show me what you can do," the father said. The little boy shuffled his feet, threw the ball up in the air, took a swing, and missed. "Strike one," said the dad.

The son repositioned his feet, threw the ball up again, took a second swing, and missed again. His father said, "Strike two."

More determined than ever, the kid dug in deeper, threw the ball higher, and took a third mighty swing. He missed again, spun completely around, and fell on the ground. His father said, "Strike three, you're out. What do you think about that?"

The youngster stood up, brushed himself off, and said, "Man, am I a good pitcher!"

2. WE NEED TO FEEL LOVED AND BE NEEDED.

There is a suicide epidemic in the world today. It affects everyone from forty-year-olds going through a midlife crisis to students in our schools. In Plano, Texas, several teenagers killed themselves in the same week. It is happening all over the country: the South Shore of New Jersey; Pine Ridge, South Dakota; Orange County, California; Dade County, Florida; Toronto, Canada.

In Iowa, there were one hundred suicide attempts in thirty days at the same high school. One girl died. The school brought Charlotte Ross, a national consultant on suicide, and Dan Clark in to talk to the kids. They split up the student body into two groups. Charlotte did the left brain, cognitive, therapy presentation. Dan did the right brain, emotional, motivational presentation. They then swapped audiences and repeated the presentations.

Finally, they gathered with counselors and healthcare professionals to interview each of the students who had attempted suicide. The demographic breakdown of those ninety-nine students was enlightening: 73 percent were on the honor roll. They said, "Thanks for the recognition, but I still have a giant hole in my heart. Something is missing in my life. Please help me!"

Six students were student-body officers elected by classmates. They said, "Thanks for letting us win a popularity contest, but I'm missing something in my life." Three students were cheerleaders. They said, "Thanks for the attention, but it's shallow and fleeting." Three students were varsity football players. They said, "We were injured. Our bodies let us down. Because we can't be athletes, we are nobody. There is nothing left."

One by one, each student told how he or she lacked "commitment relationships" in their lives. That was the phrase they used, and it caught Dan's attention. As important as the words "I love you" are to mental health and emotional stability, when it comes to commitment relationships, the words "I need you," are the most powerful words. In the context of love, people should say, "I don't love you because I need you; I need you because I love you."

Think about it. As you do, let Dan validate the deep yet elementary importance of "need" with the following example:

Dan's friend was getting married. He asked Dan to write a song and sing it at his wedding. Dan said "no." He answered, "I need you." Dan couldn't say "no" again. Dan wrote the song. Two days later, the friend phoned Dan back to explain that the band had just canceled, and he wanted Dan to prepare fifty songs to play as the dinner entertainment.

Dan emphatically said, "No way!" The friend said, "I need you." Dan couldn't say "no."

Dan practiced and prepared the music. His friend's wedding finally arrived. Dan sang the song he wrote for the couple, and sang one of the fifty others he had practiced for the dinner. Before Dan could sing another song, the band arrived. There was a miscommunication. Dan didn't want to sing all night. Dan wanted to eat and socialize like everybody else, so Dan helped the band setup their equipment.

When Dan arrived at the wedding reception, Dan arrived with the attitude that his friend needed him. Dan would have stayed until four o'clock in the morning if necessary because his friend needed him. Dan would have waited tables, mopped the floor, and contributed in any way he could. But the second the band showed up, Dan was no longer needed. In all truth, they could do without him. (We can fool others, but we can't fool ourselves.) Why hang around if he was no longer needed? Dan didn't. Dan left the reception and went home.

This is the message coming through loud and clear from adults and young people across North America, especially from those interviewed in Iowa who attempted suicide. Each one of them told Dan they knew they were liked, they knew they were loved, but they didn't believe they were needed.

The students put on a good outward show that all was well, and most of us buy into thinking outside attention and recognition motivates us. It doesn't, yet we emphasize it in our marriages, personal relationships, business contracts, and athletic endeavors. We desperately need to be needed. That's what keeps us motivated and hanging around.

The tough reality is that we can't afford to wait for someone else to tell us or show us that we are needed. It might not ever happen. We could go months before we experience this crucial validation. So, what do we do: give up and kill ourselves? No, most definitely not. Private victories must precede public victories. Who are we fooling to think it is society's responsibility to give our lives meaning, purpose, and excitement? It is our responsibility to do something on a daily basis to prove to ourselves that we are needed.

The solution then is to participate more, and be involved. We must reach out and make a move to establish, and nurture commitment relationships based on action, participation, and proactively creating symbiotic desired results.

In a relationship saying, "I need you," is not codependency. Rather, it means, "I am okay, but I would be so much more with you. You complete me." At the beginning of the wedding, Dan felt as if he was not just good, he was good for something. Dan felt that his little weird-shaped puzzle piece really did fit, that he could make a significant contribution. When the band showed up, Dan lost that understanding.

The way we recapture it, in any phase of our lives, especially in our personal and professional relationships is to change our attitude from, "What's in it for me?" to "What's in it for others?" The best way for us to prove to ourselves that we are needed is to go out of our way to lift everybody else's performance up to a higher level when we are around. Let's face it. We work harder in relationships, in sports, in church, in school, in our communities, and in everyday life when we know we make a special difference to others.

Saying "I need you" is telling them how you feel, expressing that without them, there wouldn't be everybody trying harder. More importantly, proving to yourself that you are genuinely needed is telling and showing yourself how you feel about you and your ability to make a difference in the lives of everybody you encounter. So they leave you saying, "I like me best when I'm with you, I want to see you again!"

3. ADVERSITY INTRODUCES YOU TO YOURSELF.

No one will ever know how good and smart and amazing they are until they are tested. You will never know how strong you are until being strong is your only choice!

As you know from the personal experience that my co-author shared in Chapter One, Dan played American football for thirteen years, until one day his lifelong dream of being a professional super star was taken away.

Dan's right side was pierced with the penetrating pain that felt like his body was on fire, and Dan's right arm dangled helplessly at his side.

Dan remained numb for fourteen months, and went to sixteen doctors, including Los Angeles Dodgers team physician Dr. Frank Jobe where Dan spent time at Centinela Hospital in Inglewood, California, and Craig Rehabilitation Center in Denver, Colorado where Dan underwent further tests and extensive therapy.

All sixteen doctors projected that Dan's arm would always dangle at his side, telling him he would never get any better. Sure it was a physical injury, but it affected Dan's whole life. Dan was an athlete and got a lot of attention because of it. Dan was somebody because he played football and baseball and enjoyed free food at restaurants, status at celebrity galas, fame and glory. He was going to be an overpaid NFL superstar. But in a single moment, a freak accident took away his identity. Suddenly Dan was nobody to his coaches, and nobody to his teammates and fans. Even more devastating, Dan became nobody to himself.

Dan couldn't write – He was right-handed. Dan couldn't concentrate on work or education because it constantly felt like some wild animal was biting his neck and shoulder. Needless to say, Dan hit rock bottom and life, as he knew it, was nowhere to be found. He didn't know if he even wanted to live.

Have you ever felt like that? Have you ever been so down, and confused that you thought you should leave your family, isolate yourself from friends, and contemplate checking-out altogether? Before long, Dan fell into what he thought was deep depression.

Why Dan Considered Suicide

Dan wanted to give up and contemplated suicide was because he thought he was depressed. Dan was not just paralyzed physically – Dan was also paralyzed emotionally! And what happens when you think you are depressed? You are depressed. Have you ever thought you were depressed?

With all due respect, Dan and I realize that perhaps you or a friend or loved one may have been diagnosed by a physician with a chemical imbalance, and need medication, and non-judgmental friendship, and unconditional love. We acknowledge that you (they) actually have clinical depression, and we are there for you (them!) However, through Dan's experience we also know getting better mentally and emotionally was a prerequisite to recovering physically. Dan's improvement began when he realized there is a huge difference between being depressed and being disappointed – a giant difference between being depressed and being discouraged.

When you are disappointed and discouraged you don't need medication that flat lines your emotions and dries out your human spirit to fight and survive! When Dan was paralyzed, he didn't suddenly get a chemical imbalance. Yes he was sad and experienced feeling lonely in a crowded room, and alone in a loved ones arms. But, Dan didn't need medication! What Dan needed was a change in attitude and perspective to focus on identifying his "why?" so he could again make winning personal!

Yes, Dan had some caring loved ones and associates come up to him and say, "I'm sorry. I know how you feel and what you are going through." But no they did not! No one does. Psychologists teach us that the average person talks between 100 and 200 words per minute, and yet we think between 200 and 400 words per minute. Which means, no one ever really knows everything we think, or feel, or want to say.

The author Thoreau was absolutely correct when he wrote, "Men lead lives of quiet desperation." So, what do we do? To whom do we turn? Bad and negative influences? Or good and positive influences? Bad friends or good friends? (Thank heaven Dan understood that a 'good friend' and a 'best friend' is someone who brings out the good and best in you!)

Why Didn't Dan Quit and Kill Himself?

When the final doctor told Dan that if he worked hard enough and hung in there long enough he had a chance for a 90 percent recovery, Dan believed him, which meant his 'why' was suddenly bigger than his 'why not,' and Dan recommitted to doing whatever was required to get better!

Remember, because of the way in which our bodies have been miraculously created, whenever we have injured, pulled, or broken something, as long as we go through the proper steps of rehab and required therapy, the part of our body that was injured becomes stronger than it was before we injured it!

Conclusion: Clearly, this football injury is one of the best things that ever happened to Dan. Don't misunderstand. The paralyzing accident isn't one of the best things that have happened to Dan – but what he learned about life, and priorities, and who he has become as a man, as a result of going through this setback, makes it one of the best things that have ever happened to him. Thankfully Dan now knows that when you make winning personal, you can turn every stumbling block into a stepping stone, and every setback into a comeback. Because of this, Dan is still alive to dream, and fight, and live, and laugh, and love another wonderful day!

4. EVERYBODY HURTS SOMETIME.

Everyone becomes injured sometime. So it is important that we all know that we heal in two ways: by First Intention, and by Second Intention.

We all know that doctors, and psychiatrists, and therapists can't and don't heal anyone. Through the administration of medication, the performance of surgery, and the dissemination of sound advice they help us heal ourselves. Physicians are not gods or miracle workers; they are catalysts and caregivers. With this acknowledgment let's clarify the two ways in which we heal.

Healing by the First Intention is outside-in healing where there is a scratch or superficial, shallow wound with a straight edge opening that quickly coagulates, stops bleeding, and heals with a few stitches to close the cut, or with just a Band-Aid to keep it clean. Name-calling, gossip, and rumors are "scuffed knees" and "paper cuts" that can and will always heal from the outside-in.

Healing by Second Intention is inside-out healing, where the wound is deep, the edges jagged, and the gouge uncertain. In this case, if you only stop the surface bleeding, stitch the surface layer of skin and bandage it to heal from the outside-in, underneath it all and unbeknownst to you the wound is festering, infection is setting in and gangrene could result in the amputation of that limb. When we suffer and experience a deep gouge wound – a stabbing, the bursting of our appendix, a broken heart, the loss of a loved one, a devastating divorce, being bullied at school, being let go from a job – the only way we can heal is if we keep the wound open long enough with the proper treatment – kindness and care – until it can slowly, in its own time, heal from the inside-out, one layer, one step at a time.

To conclude this chapter with an unshakable conviction that regardless of the injury or hurt, disappointment, sadness or discouragement you are experiencing, all you need to keep you positive and focused on healing is some love and support illustrated in the following tales:

"Saved By The Book"

One day, when Michael was a freshman in high school, he saw a kid from his class walking home from school. His name was Kyle. It looked like Kyle was carrying all of his books. Michael thought to himself, "Why would anyone bring home all his books on a Friday? He must really be a nerd."

Michael had quite a weekend planned (parties and a football game with his friends Saturday afternoon,) so Michael shrugged his shoulders and went on. As Michael was walking, he saw a bunch of kids running toward Kyle. They ran at him, knocking all his books out of his arms and tripping him so he landed in the dirt. His glasses went flying, and Michael saw them land in the grass about ten feet away. He looked up, and Michael saw this terrible sadness in his eyes.

Michael's heart went out to him. So, he jogged over to Kyle. As Kyle crawled around looking for his glasses, a tear fell from his eye. Michael handed him his glasses and said, "Those guys are jerks. They really should get lives." Kyle looked at Michael and said, "Hey, thanks!" There was a big smile on his face. It was one of those smiles that showed real gratitude. Michael helped him pick up his books, and asked him where he lived. As it turned out, he lived near Michael, so Michael asked him why he had never seen him before?

Kyle said he had gone to private school before now. Michael would have never hung out with a private school kid before. They talked all the way home, and Michael carried his books. Kyle turned out to be a pretty cool kid. Michael asked him if he wanted to play football on Saturday with his friends? Kyle said yes. They hung out all weekend, and the more Michael got to know Kyle, the more Michael liked him. And, Michael's friends thought the same of Kyle.

Monday morning came, and there was Kyle with the huge stack of books again. Michael stopped him and said, "Boy, you are gonna really build some serious muscles with this pile of books every day!" Kyle just laughed, and handed Michael half the books.

Over the next four years, Kyle and Michael became best friends. When they were seniors and began to think about college, Kyle decided on Georgetown. Michael was going to Duke. Michael knew that they would always be friends and that the miles would never be a problem. Kyle was going to be a doctor, and Michael was going for business on a football scholarship.

Kyle was valedictorian of their class. Michael teased him all the time about being a nerd. Kyle had to prepare a speech for graduation. Michael was so glad it wasn't him having to get up there and speak. On graduation day, Kyle looked great. He was one of those guys that really found himself during high school. He filled out and actually looked good in glasses. He had more dates than Michael did, and all the girls loved him!

Boy, sometimes Michael was jealous. Today was one of those days. Michael could see that Kyle was nervous about his speech. So, Michael smacked him on the back and said, "Hey, big guy, you'll be great!" Kyle looked at Michael with one of those looks (the really grateful one,) and smiled. "Thanks," he said.

As Kyle started his speech, he cleared his throat and began. "Graduation is a time to thank those who helped you make it through those tough years – your parents, your teachers, your siblings, maybe a coach, but mostly your friends. I am here to tell all of you that being a friend to someone is the best gift you can give them. I am going to tell you a story." With disbelief, Michael sat mesmerized as he told the story of the first day they met.

Kyle had planned to kill himself over the weekend. He talked of how he had cleaned out his locker so his mom wouldn't have to do it later, and was carrying all of his books, and the rest of his stuff home. He looked hard at Michael and gave him a little smile. "Thankfully, I was saved. My friend saved me from doing the unspeakable."

Michael heard the gasp go through the crowd as this handsome, popular boy told us all about his weakest moment. Michael saw his mom and dad looking at him, and smiling that same grateful smile. Not until that moment did Michael realize his depth. Never underestimate the power of your actions. With one small gesture, you can change a person's life.

Broken Doll

A young girl was leaving for school, and her mother reminded her to come straight home when her last class ended. Thirty minutes late, she finally walked through the front door. Her mother scolded her. "Where have you been?" she asked. "I've been worried sick." With a concerned face, the daughter sweetly replied, "I walked home with my friend, Sally, and she dropped her doll, and it broke all to pieces. It was just awful!" Her mother inquired, "So, you were late because you stayed to help her pick up the pieces of the doll and put it back together again?"

"Oh no, Mommy," she explained. "I didn't know how to fix the doll. I just stayed to help her cry!"

Remember, the promise of the universe is that everything is going to be okay in the end. If it's not okay right now, then it's not the end. So hold on for one more day – in two more days tomorrow's yesterday!

Character Challenge

I am challenging you to open up your eyes and hearts at school, and see, and feel, which students are alone a lot of the time – in the cafeteria, in the halls, on the bus. Maybe it is you that is feeling alone? Today find someone you don't know, or don't hang out with and just say the word, "Hi," with a warm smile. You never know what just one word could do to change someone's attitude, which automatically changes his/her entire day. Who knows? It might spark up a conversation that both of you needed? Write down what happened. How you felt? How it made the other person feel? What it is like to come out of your shell, and reach out to make a new friend?

The most important and critical part of this Character Challenge is to always be on the alert for anyone who mentions suicide. Take it "seriously," mention it to a trusted adult who loves them, and listens, can help them find their purpose in life again, and help them find the joy in living to the fullest – one day at a time!

DISCUSSION QUESTIONS
CHAPTER 7: THWARTING SUICIDE

1. Do you know anyone who has completed suicide? If so, who?

2. In what ways are you needed in your community, school, and home?

3. Name one trusted adult that you feel comfortable talking to if you were to have thoughts of suicide.

Chapter Eight

Character

Excellence

Excellence is something with hard work can be achieved
A quality of character that lives in you and me
Always simple, usually hard, but hard's what makes it great
Constantly improving in control of our own fate

To be great at one thing, and not care about the rest
Is wasting your potential, falling short of your true best
Don't ever stop your progress; there's always room to grow
Let's all strive to be excellent, and make the future glow.
(Copyright Alexandrea Sims 2017)

Excellence is defined as: "An essential and distinguishing attribute of something or someone; the quality of excelling; possessing good qualities in high degree; greatness—the very best."

Therefore, achieving "excellence" is never easy to do. Excellence is a quality that people really appreciate because it is so hard to find.

Getting an A+ shows excellence. Everybody knows that Michael Jordan's basketball career was filled with excellence. What many forget is his famous confession:

> "I've missed more than 9000 shots in my career. I've lost almost 300 games. 26 times, I've been trusted to take the game winning shot and missed. I've failed over and over and over again in my life. I can accept failure, everyone fails at something, but I can't accept not trying. Some people want it to happen, some wish it would happen, and others make it happen. And that is why I succeed."

Many years ago the Wall Street Journal ran this full-page motivational reminder:

> *"You've failed many times, although you may not remember.*
> *You fell down the first time you tried to walk.*
> *You almost drowned the first time you tried to swim, didn't you?*
> *Did you hit the ball the first time you swung the bat?*
> *Heavy hitters - the ones who hit the most*
> *home runs - also strike out a lot.*
> *Babe Ruth struck out 1,330 times, but he also hit 714 home runs.*
> *R. H. Macy failed seven times before his store*
> *in New York caught on. English Novelist John Creasey*
> *got 753 rejection slips before he published 564 books.*
> *Don't worry about failure. Worry about the chances*
> *you miss when you don't even try."*

Yes, we love Picasso and Shakespeare for their excellence. When you see excellence, you should appreciate the work that went into it. So much in the world falls short of excellence. Do you agree? I suppose we all do because this is what we have been taught to believe.

With your permission, I want to change this up a bit. Michael Jordan and the rest of these examples eventually succeeded and reached the highest levels of 'excellence because they 'failed their way to success." They attempted, risked, and failed more than most even try. They understood that if you are not training and pushing yourself to your ultimate capacity and potential as a human being, someone else, somewhere else, is. And when you meet him, he will win! Each of these super stars knew they had to become everything they were born to be – the very best version of themselves first, before they could successfully compete against others.

Thankfully, I too, was taught to compete against myself before I ever compete against someone else. Which means: I should never compare myself to someone else before I compare myself against myself. I have also been taught that the goal in every aspect of our existence is to achieve perfection, knowing I would never actually attain perfection, but in the process achieve excellence, and become more than I thought I could be.

Does this sound more like the way you were raised? In my experience, "best" is only relevant to what you are comparing against it. Albert Einstein said:

> "Everybody is a Genius. But If You Judge a Fish by Its Ability to Climb a Tree, It Will Live Its Whole Life Believing that It is Stupid."

For this reason, "Excellence" has to be about a constant and continual effort to become better today than we were yesterday – only striving to better our own past best personal performance – committing to becoming the very best version of ourselves physically, mentally, spiritually, emotionally, socially, financially in our recreational activities, in volunteering for a charity, and as a positive contributing member within our family and neighborhood.

The word "Excellence" is pretty self-explanatory, but what does it mean to you? You could be good at many things, but to be excellent, you must spend an extensive amount of time and energy perfecting one thing at a time until you feel that you would be proficient enough to teach it to someone else. Now, who is to say you can't be excellent at more than one thing – you absolutely can. It just means you would need to spend much of your time working on perfecting many areas of your life. When you think of someone who is an "excellent human being," what makes this someone excellent? To have excellent character, I believe we need to understand and commit to living by the Eight Keys of Excellence:

- Match behavior with values.
- Learn from mistakes.
- Speak honestly and kindly.
- Make the most of every moment.
- Take responsibility for actions.
- Be willing to do things differently.
- Get knocked down seven times - get up eight.
- Reward 'effort' before you reward results.

I also believe we greatly increase our chances of achieving "Excellence" when we focus on three key areas: Time Management, Attitude, and our desire and willingness to Stretch.

Time Management

With life there comes a constant – why are we all here
And how long will it last – we tend to ask in fear
Time's not in our hands, we can't control who comes or goes
But you control what's next, and what your future actually holds

Time is something special, you can never get it back
So use it wisely, learn, and grow, and don't stop keeping track
It's time to take control, life's just waiting to be grabbed
So never waste your time, you never know how long you have.
(Copyright Alexandrea Sims 2017)

William Shakespeare once said, "Better three hours too soon, than one minute too late." How many people do you know that are constantly late? I can think of five right off the top of my head. I am definitely not one of those people. Ever since I was a little girl, I have always had anxiety about being late, and those people who can't seem to be on time get on my last nerve. It all comes down to time management.

So what is "Time Management?" The concept is simple, plan out your day and make sure that you have plenty of time to get from point A to point B. Once you start respecting other people's time, people will also respect yours as well, and that will eliminate one huge cause of stress for many people. Tips for being on time:

- Know your goals, and all that you want to accomplish by the end of the day.

- Prioritize most important to least important. (In case life gets in the way and you can't get all of them done).

- Eliminate distractions.

- Plan ahead, set out your outfit, and any supplies you might need for the day so that it is all together and ready to go when you get up the next morning.

- Wake up ten minutes earlier. If you give yourself that extra time to awaken and get moving, you will be more likely to get ready faster and be out the door on time.

Attitude

An attitude of gratitude is happiness and light
We have a choice day in and out, to always choose what's right
And when we do, we start to see the changes from within
And somehow we begin to all feel better in our skin

Your attitude is everything, be wise with how you live
And know that we feel best when it's to others that we give
When your attitude is right, abilities will follow
And when you choose to smile, you'll be fulfilled and won't feel hollow.
(Copyright Alexandrea Sims 2017)

Have you ever wondered why people act a certain way? Do you ever look at people, and wonder what has happened to them that might be causing them to make the choices they are making? The way we act is a reflection of our attitude and the way we carry ourselves on a day-to-day basis.

Webster's Dictionary defines Attitude as: "A settled way of thinking or feeling about someone or something, typically one that is reflected in a person's behavior."

This is absolutely true. The challenge is that most of us don't realize the depth of this definition.

Zimbabwean politician Roy T. Bennett quotes, "Attitude is a choice. Happiness is a choice. Optimism is a choice. Kindness is a choice. Giving is a choice. Respect is a choice. Whatever choice you make makes you. Choose wisely."

Choose to seek "Excellence" in all you do! Good feelings and positive self-esteem don't create good behavior and desired results. Good behavior and taking action create a healthy self-image and positive self-worth. Remember, when your attitude is right, you have a better chance of being productive, feeling accomplished, having better days ahead and seeking ways and opportunities to "raise your bar."

"The Broomstick Test"

A great illustration of the kind of support we need in order to stretch is what Dan calls the "Broomstick Test." When he works with professional or amateur athletic teams, Dan will often assemble the team in their meeting room and ask a captain and an assistant coach to come to the front of the room and hold the ends of a broomstick, so it is suspended twelve inches off the floor. Ahead of time, Dan gets the name of the most naturally gifted and talented athlete on the team, (the one with the thirty-eight-inch vertical leap,) and when the broomstick is in place, Dan asks him to come forward and jump over the bar.

Dan usually finds him sitting in the back of the room, and he always hesitates and gives Dan a cocky, arrogant look like, "Hey, don't you read the newspaper? Don't you know who I am? Why are you bothering me?"

After some prodding, the athlete finally strolls up to the front of the room, walking with a swag that looks as though he had sat on something hot.

Dan then asks him if he thinks he can jump over the twelve-inch high broomstick? After he glares at Dan, conveying that this is a waste of his precious time and how dare he insult his athletic sophistication, Dan changes the question, "Will you jump over the broomstick?"

Grinning sarcastically, he skips over the bar and stares Dan down again.

In front of everyone, Dan then asks why he jumped only twelve inches high when he, and his coaches, and teammates know he can jump thirty-eight inches high?

Every time Dan has conducted this exercise in the National Football League, in the NCAA, or in an organizational retreat, the player or employee replied, "Because that is all you asked me to do."

This star player is one of the best athletes in the sport, and yet because of his contract, management often can't ask him to give more, do more, be more, or "jump higher." In business, we can't offer a raise every time we want someone to take productivity to the next level. We can't motivate military or political leaders to increase their performance with money or recognition either. We can motivate them to continue down the road toward significance only by expressing expectations – and not just any expectations, but expectations pegged to their own noble quest, their dream, their purpose.

What are your current expectations in the physical, mental, spiritual, emotional, social, financial, and familial sides of your life? How high is your bar compared to your potential? Who is stretching you? Because all the strengthening occurs in the area past the point of discomfort, and none of us can stretch ourselves to our ultimate capacity as human beings all by ourselves, we all need someone to raise our bar and, most importantly to ask us to jump!

We also must dedicate ourselves to going above and beyond the right now – even if we're afraid or otherwise resistant. Obviously we can't jump higher than we are currently able, but still we must keep jumping.

If you want to get better at doing push-ups, you get better and stronger by doing push-ups. Self-esteem, desire, and motivation are not required to change behavior. We need to change what we're doing – behavior changes behavior! When do most people fix their health problems? When it's too late. When do most people read a book on relationships? When their relationships are falling apart.

Stretching

Although deciding to stretch is a personal decision, we can stretch ourselves only so far on our own.

Stretching requires that someone not merely take us past the point of discomfort, but also support us as we hold ourselves in a zone of discomfort so that we can strengthen ourselves to the point that we don't flip back to where we were physically, mentally, spiritually, and emotionally before we started to stretch.

This process is best understood and implemented using the Vertical Stretching Scale that applies to every aspect of our lives:

10
9
8
7
6
5
4
3
2
1

Vertical Stretching Scale

Obviously, the first step is to start where we are. Next, we push and strain ourselves to the point of discomfort. Third, we ask someone we trust and respect to stretch us past the point of discomfort and support us there until the strain, and stretch is no longer stressful.

Once we have grown comfortable at the 7, 8, and 9 levels, they become our new starting points, the new normal, and on our revised amped-up scale we start again at 1.

Now the level that used to be 10 becomes level 6 - no longer the snapping point, but instead the targeted point of discomfort, which we now can handle and surpass with support. Too many of us want to stretch and strengthen all at once. Leaders, and teachers, and coaches, and parents set outrageously high, unrealistic goals without giving even a modest amount of support. Then they blame their people when they snap and fall.

I know a lot of superstar athletes, corporate executives, military leaders, and professionals in every field who will verify that all strengthening occurs in the area past the point of discomfort. While you can get to the point of discomfort on your own, you need someone else whom you admire and respect to push you past that point, and then support you there while you become stronger.

Being Stretched And Stretching Others Through Influence

This metaphor of physical therapy is at the heart and soul of what it means to be a leader. At the end of the day, what qualifies someone to be a called a leader is that person's capacity to influence others to stretch their minds (attitudes,) and behaviors in order to achieve important significant results.

Most believe the word influence is synonymous with the less impressive and more suspicious tool called persuasion. It's not. In no way is this about allowing someone to apply the right combination of verbal tricks to get us to change, or to equip us as fast talking manipulators who use stealthy tactics to exert our will over others.

Stretching is about making winning personal, and influencing yourself and others to take the required and necessary steps to get from where you are to where you want to be, regardless of the effort or how long it takes.

The good news is that in order to create profound and lasting change, you don't have to stretch fifty behaviors. You usually have to stretch only one or two key behaviors and leverage them. This means stretching is more than focusing on vague results, such as "Create a culture of excellence," or "Help troubled teenagers," or "Build a winning team."

Stretching is having a clear determination of what specific behaviors are needed to change, and having a clear understanding of what strategies to implement in order to actually change those behaviors.

Become More Of Who You Already Are

The incredible courage shown by tiny, tenacious Kari Strug in the 1996 Olympic Games in Atlanta, Georgia, reminds us all about the powerful cliché "Proper prior planning prevents poor performance." It also reminds us that both physical and mental toughness are required to be a champion.

As a very young gymnast I remember my coach gathering our team together one day and showing us a short video of her self when she was our age. Her name was Missy Marlowe, and she had competed on the U.S. Olympic gymnastics team in 1988. She was also named one of the prestigious 'Top Six' best male and female athletes in the United States—and received the Broderick Award as the NCAA Outstanding Female Athlete of the Year.

This video showed Missy as a little girl receiving instruction on the uneven parallel bars, trying to execute a difficult maneuver. I watched her crash to the mat ten times in a row. After the tenth fall, she sobbed and limped away, but it didn't stop her. She came back, and I watched her fall four more times, each time smashing hard into the mat. Finally, on the fifteenth try, Missy spun off the high bar, reached out, grabbed the lower bar, spun around to catch the high bar again and completed the maneuver.

When the video had ended Coach Missy explained that every new girl goes through the same thing to learn each one of the many difficult moves required to win meets and impress judges. She also pointed out that nobody clapped that day. There were no cameras to record her victory. Only her face showed personal satisfaction. And when she eventually won the NCAA national championship in the all-around competition, the hard work, sacrifice, and painful endurance were all worth it.

Great story, eh? But the most memorable part was when she asked us if we would have quit on the first fall? Or given up after the fifth or the ninth fall, rationalizing that surely we had given it our best effort and no one could expect any more? Coach then asked the scariest question of all: What if you had quit on the fourteenth fall, not realizing that just one more attempt would make the difference between failure and success – between settling for average and being a national champion?

The next time you see a super star in any field I hope you'll remember that any great achievement in life requires hours of lonely, deliberate preparation, relentless effort and hard work. Don't make the mistake of thinking that athletes, teachers, counselors, coaches, artists, doctors, attorneys, scientists, writers, or actors didn't spend years learning how to perform in their areas of expertise. You can be sure they paid their dues in time, effort, solitude, and in getting back up on their 'bars' every time they fell until they eventually achieved their goal.

Who are you? What do you think you can do right now to become more of who you already are?

Character Challenge

It's been said that, "inspired people don't have to be motivated." It's also a proven fact that passion drives performance, and once we identify our "why?" for doing something, figuring out the "how?" becomes clear and simple. Make a list of the many different activities you are involved in right now? Which one are you the most passionate about? Now commit to spending an extra 10 minutes a day, working on it for one week. At the end of the week, write down what you have improved on. How does it make you feel to see a positive physical and emotional/motivational change in yourself?

Remember, success breeds success. As you continue to keep this commitment, you will achieve excellence in the thing that you are working on. Once you have mastered your first one, then move onto the next hobby/activity that you enjoy and follow the same pattern. It's only a matter of time before you reach and feel excellent in every area of your life.

DISCUSSION QUESTIONS
CHAPTER 8: EXCELLENCE

1. What is the difference between excellence and mastery?

2. Why is it important to compare yourself to you before comparing yourself to anyone else?

3. Look at the Eight Keys of Excellence. Which one do you do really well? Which one could you improve on?

4. What does "Whatever choice you make makes you" mean to you?

5. How are you currently being stretched?

6. What changes behavior?

7. Before we identify our "why", what do we need to determine?

Chapter Nine
Character
Resiliency

How do you react when you fall down or lose the race
Do you stay down and wallow in the dirt in self-disgrace
Or, do you quickly brush it off, and then move right along
And then bounce back, and rise above the failure and the wrong

Take your losses in, and always find the lesson learned
You'll keep on rising to the top, and no bridges will burn
Just know if it is meant to be, the world will all be yours
When you fall down, get right back up, and grace those open doors.
(Copyright Alexandrea Sims 2017)

RESILIENCY IS DEFINED as: "The capacity to recover quickly from difficulties; toughness; the ability of a substance or object to spring back into shape; elasticity."

How many times in your life have you felt like giving up? Felt as though the whole world was against you and there was no way you were going to make it to the finish line? That happens to me daily...

literally daily. Being resilient is one of the most important lessons I learned as a young girl.

When I was five-years-old, I taught myself how to ride a bike. No training wheels, or help from Mom or Dad, I was determined to get that bike up and moving on my own.

As a little kid with no skill of bike riding, I crashed and burned for hours – getting scraped and bruised all over my body. I refused to come inside, until I could tell my parents what I had accomplished.

This resilient fire inside of me has stayed with me my entire life, and I'm so grateful for always being able to bounce back from failure. I truly believe resilience is a major key to having great character. If you have the ability to quickly move on, and learn from your mistakes, you will find much success in life.

As a professional dancer, I audition for twice as many jobs as I receive. I attend an audition almost every single day; and nine times out of ten I do not get the job. I ask myself each time, why I chose this life? The life of living paycheck-to-paycheck, never knowing if I'm going to succeed, or not. So, why do I do it?

It all comes down to "Resiliency." I know that no matter how many times I get knocked down, if I continue to push through and keep working hard, all of my wildest dreams will someday come true. I have now lived in Los Angeles for six years and though I have found much success as a dancer, it doesn't change the fact that I still get turned down more often than I am hired.

What would have happened if I had not mastered the art of resiliency and just given up not booking nine auditions in a row? If I did not attend that tenth audition, I would not have booked my first world tour with Latin artist **Chayanne**, and I would not have been able to live my dream of traveling around the world getting paid to dance.

There have been so many dark days where I felt like less than nothing, like the most untalented person in the world. Feeling, I am not good enough. On those days, all I want to do is crawl into a hole of depression and never come out. It has never been in my nature to be depressed, but this choice of profession has tested me more than

I would ever choose to admit. So, how do I bounce back? I cling to the hope that I'm going to have another audition, and once again be living out my dreams on stage.

Even after six years of success at the highest level of my profession, I often still feel like a failure, but I have learned to get back up and always go again, and therefore I am able to still be living out my dancing dreams today.

CREATING SELF

Obviously, "Creating Self" is a process that never ends because of self-actualization, and becoming predictably significant is an everlasting work in progress. To help us sustain our motivation to continually stretch and improve, we need to surround ourselves with others of like mind and who seek similar desired results. To find and attract those of like mind, first requires that we know what we believe when it comes to dealing with our trials, tests, and tribulations, or how we need to think and respond when they occur.

One evening during a conversation with some friends, one girl expressed her concern about her little sister. Her exact words were, "She needs to find herself." In the next few minutes our discussion revealed a different reality that has changed my perspective forever. 'Self' is not discovered – self is created.

No one can 'find' them selves. We already 'are.' As the song says, "No matter where you go, there you are. A geographic relocation doesn't change much." Yet how many people go on 'pilgrimages' in search of themselves, believing in some strange way that they can pull up to a bus stop and suddenly 'meet' themselves, exclaiming, "where have you been my entire life?"

In a humorous observation, we laughed about the most popular places that people go to find themselves, including Santa Fe, New Mexico and Boulder, Colorado, where on any given day you can see people walking in the mountains with back-pack's on looking for themselves. They act like they can play 'hide-and-go-seek' calling out, "I see you – come out from behind that tree and reveal yourself!"

Because self is created, no matter what your past has been you have a spotless future. Because self is created, it is necessary that we also understand that our perspective is created – that perception is reality. Therefore, let us never set ourselves up for failure by seeing ourselves in a negative light. For example, if you see yourself in the mirror as overweight, out of shape, and label yourself as a 'fat failure,' does this lend itself to an attitude of change and personal improvement? Absolutely not!

How simple and powerful and yes humorous it would be if you changed your attitudinal perspective from a 'fat failure' to someone who has been very successful at putting on weight? You did not gain your weight all at once. You gained it one pound, one calorie at a time, which means you can and must lose it one pound, one calorie at a time. In every circumstance, negative self and positive self are both created. Which will you choose?

Welcoming And Regulating Stress

Have you ever noticed how some people, even "the best" players, who practice and practice to become brilliant at the basics, still choke come game time?

Do you know anyone who has stretched from the inside out and has truly become more of who they already are and yet when it comes time to perform, and show what they can do, they fold under pressure taking a school test or playing in a big game?

Have you noticed how stress even affect some "right" leaders, coaches and players, teachers, parents and students, but seemingly not others? Why do you think this occurs?

When the external circumstance is the same for everybody competing and involved, it is clear that stress is the only thing that can be controlled to a high degree. Research produced the well-known Yerkes-Dodson Law, diagramed below:

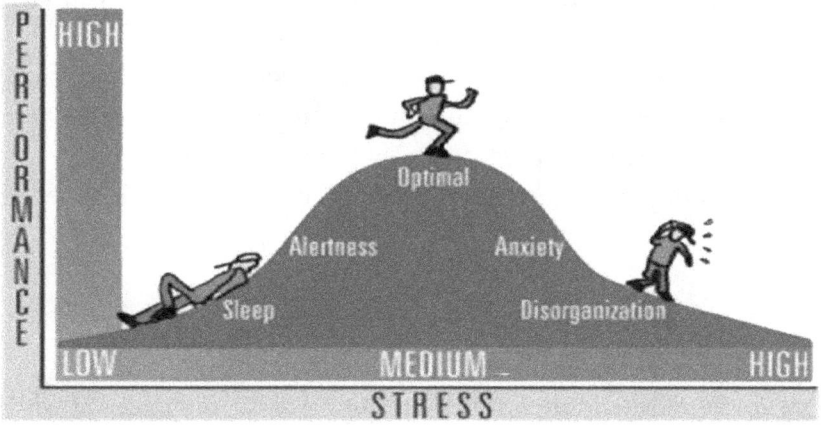

From this diagram, it is obvious and extremely important to remember that stress and performance are always linked. Stress facilitates performance. Too little stress causes weak performance. However, too much stress is debilitating. Peak performance comes as we seek balance. We must seek the optimal level of stress.

Surely we are all different in how much stress we can handle. The goal is to push to our highest degree of intensity, so that we may perform at our ultimate capacity and reach our full potential. But how will we know when we have gone past the level of optimal stress?

It's about the simple law of diminishing returns. We can water a tomato plant only so much. At full capacity, when the plant needs no more water additional watering only diminishes its growth. Once the water level reaches an optimal level, the effectiveness of water quickly diminishes and eventually kills the tomato plant.

Stress is not what happens to you.
It is your reaction or response to what happens.
A reaction is negative and uncontrolled.
A response is positive and something we choose to control.

As already mentioned, pressure is not something that is naturally there. It is created when you question your own ability. When you know what you can do, there is no question. Even when you know you are over your head, pressure is not stress.

The internal impact that stress has on an individual physically and mentally varies among individuals and plays a huge role in performance level. In competition, talent and experience don't explain differences in performance. The one and only thing we can control is stress.

When Stress Is Bad

If you're worried about your health, stop. Worry only makes it worse. Warning signs of pushing ourselves past the optimal level of stress include heartburn, appetite changes, irritable bowl, itchy skin, nervous habits such as nail biting, talking way too fast and way too much, insomnia, headaches, chest pain, high blood pressure, high cholesterol, and an increase in drug and alcohol use.

Performance-related signs are even more obvious and noticeable, including decreased concentration, resulting in increased errors.

Because these conditions drain our energy, stress simultaneously tells other costly physical processes – including digestion, physical growth, and some aspects of the immune system – to shut down or slow down, making us more susceptible to illnesses ranging from the common cold to cancer. Chronic stress has been linked to heart disease, strokes, depression, Type 2 diabetes, and Post Traumatic Stress.

When Stress Is Good

The good news is that every one of these negative conditions can be avoided or at least positively managed through proper diet, exercise, rest, and a personal commitment to take positive action. Even when we experience physical injury and pain.

For example, Dan has had his head sewn up eleven times, has broken his neck, nose, jaw, right arm, left wrist, all the bones in his left hand, both thumbs, both pinky fingers, has had two hernias, and his appendix burst in the hospital. In addition to all that, Dan has battled throat cancer, snapped both patella tendons, severed his left Achilles tendon, and has torn the cartilage/ligaments in his left ankle, and both knees – all requiring multiple surgeries and many plaster casts.

Our Point? Every single time Dan was injured, he has fully recovered. Because he religiously followed and obeyed the time-tested rehabilitation program prescribed for him, the injured part of his body became stronger than it was before the injury – including his broken heart!

> *Two predominant 'red flag' predictors of suicide are giving up and isolation.*

Which means the right meaningful treatment that reveals both a need to keep keeping on and instills a sense of connection — two of the most important things that all of us need - will always turn our bad stress into good stress.

FINDING THE OPPORTUNITY IN PERSONAL CHANGE

Richard Nelson, a sixteen-year-old junior at Manti High School in Utah, was an outstanding athlete. He was the number-two singles player on the state championship tennis team and had just made the basketball team that would go on that year to win the state championship. He was looking forward to much success as a senior during the following season. But on October 23, 1966, most of his athletic future was suddenly taken away from him.

That night, Richard was riding his bicycle from Manti to Gunnison to visit his girlfriend. The road was very steep in some places, which allowed Richard to reach speeds of forty miles per hour on the downhill slopes. Because it was dark and difficult to see, Richard was following the white line on the shoulder of the road to ensure his safety. As he came around a blind curve and was looking down at the ground, Richard failed to see a parked car jacked up to fix a flat tire on his side of the road. With no warning, he hit the parked car and ended up in the hospital where he didn't regain consciousness for two days. Besides bad cuts on his head and knee, he broke his collarbone and right arm. He wore an L-shaped cast on his arm for two months.

When the cast came off on December 29, Richard's doctor gave him a series of tests to determine the success of his healing. Richard failed all the tests. His triceps muscle had lost all its strength – he could not push out with his arm. The doctor diagnosed a pinched nerve and said that Richard might never regain the use of his right arm. Richard's once strong, but now puny right arm just hung at his side and the doctor gave him no real hope of recovery.

Because of his injury, Richard wasn't able to play on the basketball team during the rest of that year, but the coach made him equipment and statistics manager so that he could come to practice and be around the guys on the team.

His junior year ended, the summer came, and Richard was determined to do whatever he had to do to make the basketball team the next year. He realized that he couldn't make it right-handed, so he started working on his left-handed skills.

All summer long, each and every night, he practiced making left-handed baskets at the outdoor courts in the center of town. Every night, he shot two hundred left-handed baskets and practiced left-handed dribbling and passing off the park retaining wall. Instead of going with his friends to the summer dances sponsored by the high school, Richard practiced basketball.

When the next season arrived, Richard was ready to try out for the team – and he made it! He never became a starter, but he was always the first substitute to go in the game.

The season boiled down to the final game of the year against their archrival, Richfield High. This game would determine which team would win the league championship and advance to the state tournament playoffs. It was a "must win" for both teams.

On Friday night, the gym was packed. The starting guard for Manti had sprained his ankle earlier in the week, so Richard finally got his big break – he started the game! However, before the first quarter was over Richard was replaced. It was hard to compete when he could only use one arm. The game continued until the last thirty seconds when Manti's other guard was injured, forcing Richard back into the game. Richfield was ahead by three points and Manti had the ball.

The Richfield team's coach tried to take advantage of the situation by having one of his players immediately foul Richard. Undaunted, Richard stepped up to the free throw line. (If he made the first foul shot, he would get a chance to shoot and make a second basket.) Confidently, Richard picked up the ball, braced it in his left hand and shot. Swish! He made it, and the crowd went wild! He then made the next shot, bringing Manti High to within one point of Richfield. The crowd stood and went crazy again!

Richfield then took the ball out of bounds and threw a long pass down court to the player Richard was guarding, trying to make a quick, easy basket. But Richard, with his undying determination, leaped through the air to intercept the pass.

When he landed, he was fouled again and was given another opportunity at the free throw line. With ten seconds left on the clock, Richard balanced the ball in his left hand, took a deep breath, and shot. The crowd was deathly quiet until – swish! He tied the game! His next shot went up, down and through. Swish again!

He made it – he made all four shots – left-handed! Richard Nelson won the game and became the hero of the school.

According to Richard Nelson, he was not a hero. "Anybody could have done what I did," he said in his postgame interview. "I was supposed to make those shots. Everybody was counting on me to win the game when I was put in that situation. All I did was believe in myself, work hard when others didn't and persevere. Anybody could have done what I did in the game if they had shot as many foul shots as I had shot last summer in practice."

As Earl Nightingale said, "The only difference between a successful person and an unsuccessful person is that the successful person will do what the unsuccessful person will not do. The key is the successful person does not want to do it either, but then does it anyway."

Character Challenge

Think of something this week that did not go your way. Was it a test in school that did not go as well as you had hoped? Or, have you lost a game? Be honest with exactly how it made you feel and think about how it affected you. Now write down below a coping mechanism that you may not have thought of in the heat of the moment, but could have helped you bounce back a little bit quicker than you initially did. Once you identify the way in which you choose to deal with things, only then will you be able to dig down deep and work on handling each and every situation in a better, more positive manner.

DISCUSSION QUESTIONS
CHAPTER 9: RESILIENCY

1. Peak performance comes with what level of stress?

2. How do you know when you have gone past your optimal stress level?

3. Define stress.

4. What can you do to physically manage your stress better?

5. How can your mindset affect your stress?

6. Can someone else make us feel bad? Why or why not?

7. What is the difference between a successful person and unsuccessful person to you?

The End
(Which Is The Beginning)

Former U.S. President Ronald Reagan summarizes what happens to us as individuals and to us as a collective nation of proud Americans, when we become people of Character. His challenge:

> *"What makes us Americans different? We've always reached for a new spirit and aimed at a higher goal. We've been courageous and determined, unafraid and bold. Who among us wants to be first to say we no longer have those qualities - that we must limp along doing the same things that have brought us our present misery? It's time to chart a new course, to meet the great challenge, to reach beyond the commonplace and not fall short for lack of creativity or courage. And to do this? All we need to begin with is a dream that we can do better than before. All we need to have is faith, and that dream will come true. All we need to do is act, and the time for action is now."*

Dan and I invite you to join us in accepting this challenge to all Americans; to always be Aware of the significance of Character, that each of us may embrace the nine qualities, attitudes, attributes and traits illuminated in the acronym C.H.A.R.A.C.T.E.R. and live them every day of our lives!

Character Awareness

CHARACTER AWARENESS is the new book on your shelf
Take time to re-read it and evaluate yourself
Are you looking forward cause success is there to take
Having CLARITY in all the choices that you make

Are you being truthful, kind and patient when you speak
HONESTY is necessary all days of the week
Are you treating others as you wish they would treat you
Let's be ANTI-BULLIES and stick up for others too

When you make a choice regardless if it's bad or good
Do you take RESPONSIBILITY just like you should
Are there things in life you cannot seem to live without
If it's an ADDICTION seek some help without a doubt

It's crucial to find balance from one day into the next
CONSISTENCY you need if you are going to be your best
If you're feeling hopeless, disconnected without love
THWART all SUICIDAL thoughts - you're needed and you're loved!

When striving to be EXCELLENT there is no room for breaks
We must be consistent in pursuit of being great
Let us learn from our mistakes and strengthen where we lack
RESILIENCY is knowing deep inside we can bounce back

So take these tips and start to make improvements day by day
And you will see your Character improve in every way

About The Author

Alexandrea Sims, originally from Salt Lake City, Utah, was a state champion and nationally recognized gymnast, and has been living and working in Los Angeles since she graduated from high school in 2011.

Alexandrea is an accomplished artist, writer, poet, model, actress, musician, dancer, choreographer, teacher, and successful business entrepreneur. As a professional dancer, she has completed two world tours performing with Latin superstar Chayanne, and has worked for other artists including Pharrell Williams, Robin Thicke, Missy Elliot, Meghan Trainor, Natalie La Rose, Flo Rida, Montel Jordan, actor Hugh Jackman and more. Alexandrea has performed at the Billboard Music Awards, BET awards, iHeart Radio Music Awards, Latin Billboard Awards, on the Tribute To Julie Andrews, and in between performing and traveling currently works with new up and coming artists as a dancer, concept producer and confidant.

As a model Alexandrea has been featured on the cover of a popular video game, and has appeared in many national commercials for companies such as Chrysler, FX, Ubisoft, Just Dance, Shake Weight, Dentrix and Sara Lee. Alexandrea has also been featured in international billboard and print campaigns around the world for Alexander McQueen, MAC Cosmetics, Hot Tuna Swimwear, Maggie Sottero, Alyse's Bridal, Ubisoft and Mrs. Fields Cookies.

As an actress Alexandrea has appeared on the TV shows Glee and Hit The Floor and in the movie High School Musical.

As an author Alexandrea has written 26 children's books, a book of Lyrical Poetry, and proudly presents this book on Character Awareness as her contribution to help young men and women make better choices and control their manifest destiny. Committed to being a life-long-learner, and aware of her responsibility to be a good, clean, positive, productive, powerful role model and advocate for youth, Alexandrea can't wait to see where her dreams, passion and drive will take her in the near and distant future!

Co-Author

Dan Clark is founder and CEO of the international communications firm Dan Clark and Associates; University Professor; High Performance Business Coach; National Talk Radio Host; Award Winning Athlete; Gold Record Songwriter; New York Times Best Selling Author of 34 books; and a primary contributing author to the Chicken Soup For The Soul series who has been published in more than 50 million books, in 40 languages.

Between 1983 and 1989, Dan was invited by Mrs. Nancy Reagan to create a school assembly program to take her "Just Say No" message to students in all 50 states.

Dan has been inducted into the National Speakers Hall of Fame, named one of the Top Ten Motivational Speakers In The World, has spoken to over 5500 audiences, to millions of people, in 61 countries, on 6 continents, is the proud father of four amazing and significant children, and in 2012 was honored as Utah Father of the Year. Dan speaks primarily at corporate conventions with a continued passion to keynote state and national educator conferences, Coaches clinics and PTSA meetings around the country.

www.ingramcontent.com/pod-product-compliance
Lightning Source LLC
Chambersburg PA
CBHW031646040426
42453CB00006B/224